W9-ATZ-737

ENHANCING
RTI

ASCD MEMBER BOOK

Many ASCD members received this book as a
member benefit upon its initial release.

Learn more at: **www.ascd.org/memberbooks**

ENHANCING RTI

How to Ensure Success with
Effective Classroom Instruction & Intervention

Douglas Fisher | Nancy Frey

Alexandria, Virginia USA

ASCD

1703 N. Beauregard St. • Alexandria, VA 22311-1714 USA
Phone: 800-933-2723 or 703-578-9600 • Fax: 703-575-5400
Web site: www.ascd.org • E-mail: member@ascd.org
Author guidelines: www.ascd.org/write

Gene R. Carter, *Executive Director;* Nancy Modrak, *Publisher;* Scott Willis, *Director, Book Acqui-sitions & Development;* Julie Houtz, *Director, Book Editing & Production;* Jamie Greene, *Editor;* Catherine Guyer, *Senior Graphic Designer;* Mike Kalyan, *Production Manager;* Valerie Younkin, *Typesetter;* Sarah Plumb, *Production Specialist*

Printed in the United States of America. Cover art © 2010 by ASCD. ASCD publications present a variety of viewpoints. The views expressed or implied in this book should not be interpreted as official positions of the Association.

All Web links in this book are correct as of the publication date below but may have become inactive or otherwise modified since that time. If you notice a deactivated or changed link, please e-mail books@ascd.org with the words "Link Update" in the subject line. In your message, please specify the Web link, the book title, and the page number on which the link appears.

ASCD Member Book, No. FY10-7 (May 2010, P). ASCD Member Books mail to Premium (P), Select (S), and Institutional Plus (I+) members on this schedule: Jan., PSI+; Feb., P; Apr., PSI+; May, P; July, PSI+; Aug., P; Sept., PSI+; Nov., PSI+; Dec., P. Select membership was formerly known as Comprehensive membership.

PAPERBACK ISBN: 978-1-4166-0987-2   ASCD product #110037

Also available as an e-book (see Books in Print for the ISBNs).

Quantity discounts for the paperback edition only: 10–49 copies, 10%; 50+ copies, 15%; for 1,000 or more copies, call 800-933-2723, ext. 5634, or 703-575-5634. For desk copies: member@ascd.org.

Library of Congress Cataloging-in-Publication Data
Fisher, Douglas, 1965-
  Enhancing RTI : how to ensure success with effective classroom instruction and intervention / Douglas Fisher & Nancy Frey.
      p. cm.
  Includes bibliographical references and index.
  ISBN 978-1-4166-0987-2 (pbk. : alk. paper)
 1. Remedial teaching—United States.   2. Slow learning children—Education—United States. 3. Learning disabled children—Education—United States.   4. Effective teaching—United States. 5. Classroom management—United States.   I. Frey, Nancy, 1959–   II. Title.
  LB1029.R4F48 2010
  372.43—dc22
                                                                                                    2009053850

20 19 18 17 16 15 14   4 5 6 7 8 9 10 11 12

Enhancing RTI

How to Ensure Success with Effective Classroom Instruction and Intervention

Acknowledgments

This book has taken us our entire careers to write. We have so many people to acknowledge. Early on, we were influenced by our colleagues interested in inclusive school practices for students with disabilities, especially the Florida Inclusion Network and Barbara Buswell of PEAK Parent Center (www.peakparent.org). In addition, we were privileged to learn alongside teachers in the City Heights Collaborative—Rosa Parks Elementary School, Monroe Clark Middle School, and Hoover High School—for nearly a decade. The collaborative allowed us to try out many of the ideas in this book with actual students and teachers. Of late, we have had the opportunity to work with two amazing educational systems: the Chula Vista Elementary School District, and specifically Dr. John Nelson, provided us with an opportunity to take these ideas to scale; and Health Sciences High and Middle College (HSHMC), our educational home, ensured that we keep it real on a daily basis. We thank both the teachers at HSHMC and the leadership team, especially Dr. Ian Pumpian and Sheri North, for providing daily experiences with an amazing collection of students.

Quite frankly, this book wouldn't exist without the support of the staff of ASCD and the guidance we received from Scott Willis and his team. Finally, we appreciate the professional organizations that first published our work and then allowed us to mold that work into this book. More specifically, parts of this book are drawn from the following sources:

Fisher, D., & Frey, N. (2001). *Responsive curriculum design in secondary schools: Meeting the diverse needs of students*. Lanham, MD: Scarecrow Education.

Fisher, D., & Frey, N. (2008). Releasing responsibility. *Educational Leadership, 66*(3), 32–37.

Fisher, D., Grant, M., Frey, N., & Johnson, C. (2007). Taking formative assessments schoolwide. *Educational Leadership, 65*(4), 64–68.

Fisher, D., & Ivey, G. (2006). Evaluating the interventions for struggling adolescent readers. *Journal of Adolescent & Adult Literacy, 50*, 180–189.

Frey, N. (2006). The role of 1:1 individual instruction in reading. *Theory into Practice, 45*(3), 207–214.

Introduction

We can all think of a time when we struggled in school to learn a particular skill or content area. Why did we struggle? What occurred to eventually help us overcome our obstacle to learning? In most cases, we were helped by a teacher who identified our instructional needs and then implemented one or more interventions to which we successfully responded. The result of that instruction and intervention was that we were able to improve our academic performance and self-efficacy.

The key to helping all children learn literacy and content is to believe in their ability to learn and then to explicitly guide their learning through systematic and intentional instruction and intervention. This approach combines continuous, "on-the-spot" evaluation of a learner's needs and his or her response to the implementation of evidence-based intervention strategies. If a child's response to the intervention is successful, a positive change in learning will occur. If no change in learning occurs, the teacher needs to further study the child and the initial intervention, instructional delivery, and materials. Based on new insights, the teacher can then plan a different treatment or intervention targeted to meet the child's needs.

This cycle—from assessment to instruction—enables teachers to observe students' responsiveness to the targeted interventions and to proceed with instruction that is supported by ever-evolving performance data. This Response to Instruction and Intervention (RTI^2) system is designed to change learner performance as a function of targeted instruction. The use of the RTI^2 model is desperately needed to ensure that equal access to learning is available for every child.

In the past, challenging content was reserved for the highest-achieving students. Struggling learners were excluded from chemistry, physics, and advanced history classes and were instead tracked into general science classes or classes on practical economics. Deprived of the opportunity to delve into complex ideas, many students failed to develop the higher-level thinking skills that were fostered in the more challenging classes. Unfortunately, there was also a widespread belief that not all students could learn complex information. Current evidence suggests that with the appropriate instruction and intervention, virtually every student is capable of learning challenging content. The adage that "children learn what they are taught" especially rings true when instruction and interventions are in line with identified needs.

Teaching every child is hard work. With that hard work, though, comes a group of learners who are prepared to participate in society. This learning occurs in the classrooms of well-prepared teachers who are undaunted by student learning variations because they believe that each child is an individual and that individuals exhibit differences in growth due to many factors, including carefully selected instructional interventions. The intent of this book is to provide teachers with the knowledge and tools they need to implement a Response to Instruction and Intervention system in order to realize educational outcomes in line with the belief that all children can learn.

1

Choose Your Adventure:

How RTI^2 Affects the Educational Environment

Remember the series of "choose your own adventure" books that were popular in the 1980s? They offered decision points at key moments in the story, and the choice you made determined the outcome of the tale (and often the fate of the characters). With that in mind, let's play the school version of *Choose Your Adventure*.

Adam is in the 5th grade in a public school somewhere in the United States. Here are some things to know about Adam: He is an active 10-year-old boy who plays baseball in the local Little League. He has an older sister who generally regards him as a bother (she's 13, after all) but loves him, nonetheless. Before his mother and father adopted him at the age of 7, he lived in foster care for a time with a member of his father's family. Adam's mom and dad first got to know him this way and soon decided that Adam needed to be a permanent part of their family.

Adam's family is moving to another state because his mother accepted a job offer with better pay and benefits. They plan to enroll Adam in school and prepare him by touring the school with him, introducing him to teachers, and filling out all the forms with emergency contact information, known allergies, and the like. They were delighted to learn that the school system in the new state operates on a year-round schedule, with evenly distributed breaks of three or four weeks each quarter. His parents will be adding their names to the list of school volunteers, and Adam's dad is willing to be a guest speaker at the school's career day and discuss his work in the health care field.

Here's the key moment in the story where your choice factors in and may help determine the outcome:

• If you decide to send Adam to a traditional school, your adventure begins here on page 4.

• If you decide to send Adam to a school that offers a Response to Intervention (RTI) approach, turn to page 5.

• If you decide to send Adam to a school that uses a Response to Instruction and Intervention (RTI^2) approach, turn to page 7.

The Traditional School: "What's Wrong with Adam?"

After meeting the important people in the school (the principal, the custodian, and the lunch staff), Adam settles into his 5th grade class. His teacher, Ms. Riley, is experienced with this age group and has been a staff member at the school for 15 years. Adam likes his new class and soon establishes social relationships with his peers. He is quickly seen as an asset in any recess game and is well liked by other children, who say he is "nice."

The reading block is his least favorite time of day. He stumbles over words when Ms. Riley asks him to read aloud to the class, and his handwritten work is difficult to read. She notices that during some lessons, Adam gets boisterous and calls out to other students. He is scolded frequently for his outbursts and is already becoming a regular visitor to the principal's office—not the relationship he imagined when he first met her. Adam is soon placed in a remedial reading group named the Blasters, and he spends most of the reading block in the company of a paraprofessional who works with this group in another room to minimize distractions. They complete lots of workbook pages and worksheets, but they rarely spend much time with longer books.

Adam's incomplete assignments, missed homework, and mediocre written work soon take a toll. Two marking periods later, Adam is performing well below other students in the class, and Ms. Riley calls in Adam's parents for a conference. She informs them that Adam is in danger of being retained because he hasn't received passing marks in most subjects. Following the district policy, Ms. Riley draws up a learning contract that states that, because retention is a possibility, Adam is required to attend intersession, a mandatory two-week remediation period for struggling students. Adam and his family are discouraged because they won't be able to travel and visit family during this time, but they agree that anything that might help Adam be successful is worth the sacrifice.

Adam's social relationships also begin to fray. Because classmates increasingly view him as a problem (they have, after all, witnessed their teacher dealing with him this way), they begin to avoid him. Even his physical skills are not enough to overcome difficult relationships with peers. As Adam becomes marginalized, his behavior grows more problematic, and despite the attention of the paraprofessional, Adam's reading and writing do not seem to improve. The handwriting worksheets he completes have little effect, and he daydreams more often, missing more instruction. Countless meetings later, Ms. Riley brings Adam's name to the attention of the school's Student Study Team. "I've tried everything," she tells them, and they nod in sympathetic agreement. They've seen Adam on the playground, in the chair outside the principal's office, and taking a circuitous route to the bathroom. "What's wrong with this kid?" she asks.

The team completes the paperwork for special education testing, and Adam's parents sign it. They are concerned that he is not doing well and that their once outgoing boy is withdrawing into himself. Going to school has become a daily battle, and Adam's parents are at a loss as to how to deal with him. In the meantime, Adam must now attend mandatory six-week summer school. If he is unable to do so, he will repeat 5th grade with a new set of classmates.

Adam barely passes summer school and advances to the 6th grade. By this point, his special education testing results are in. Unfortunately, Adam doesn't meet the criteria for a handicapping condition. "I guess he's just a 'flatliner,'" remarks Ms. Riley. "I hope the 6th grade teachers know what to do with him. I tried everything." The 6th grade team members, resentful that he didn't qualify for special education, are bracing themselves. "We've all seen him around school," remarks Ms. Colón. "Wish us luck."

The RTI School: "How Can We Help Adam?"

After meeting the important people in the school (the principal, the custodian, and the lunch staff), Adam settles into his 5th grade class. His teacher, Ms. Riley, is experienced with this age group and has been a staff member at the school for 15 years. Adam likes his new class and soon establishes social relationships with his peers. He is quickly seen as an asset in any recess game and is well liked by other children, who say he is "nice."

The reading block is his least favorite part of the day. His teacher used some simple screening instruments on his first day, including the San Diego Quick (LaPray & Ross, 1969), a word list that targets decoding skills, and a cloze assessment on simple machines that was based on a recent chapter from the science textbook. Ms. Riley knows that these screening instruments should not be used as factors in big decisions, but they provide a starting point for making initial instructional decisions. The results of the decoding assessment show that Adam is decoding at about a 3rd grade level. In addition, he struggled to complete the cloze assessment, accurately completing only 36 percent of the words and indicating that he had difficulty comprehending the passage. Ms. Riley knows that the next round of benchmark testing will occur in a few weeks, and this will offer a better opportunity to measure Adam's reading ability.

During the next few weeks, Ms. Riley has a chance to witness Adam's reading firsthand. While most of the reading instruction in her class comes from a core textbook, she has many books available in the class. Adam seems to drift from book to book when the class is engaged in independent reading time. Ms. Riley offers to help him locate books of interest, but to no avail. Adam consistently abandons books after a few pages, spending most of his time "looking" for a new book to read.

In the meantime, the results of the benchmark assessment are clear—Adam is reading well below his peers. Fortunately, the elementary school has a Response to Intervention program. Ms. Riley contacts the Title I teacher, Mr. Alonzo, who coordinates Tier 2 supplemental interventions for 4th and 5th grade. Three times a week, several students from these two grades meet with Mr. Alonzo for additional instruction. Adam's group is rarely larger than four students, and the lesson format is always the same: begin with a flashcard game to practice decoding, read a short informational or narrative passage that matches group members' reading level, discuss the content, and respond to comprehension questions. If there's enough time, they also do a bit of writing. Adam's handwriting is difficult to read, but the intervention lesson format really doesn't allow for additional instruction in writing.

Within the next few weeks, Mr. Alonzo and Ms. Riley meet with Adam's parents. They share their concerns about Adam's current reading status and describe the intervention they have implemented. Mr. Alonzo has collected further assessment data about Adam's progress and has already charted Adam's results from the flashcard drills and his rate of accuracy for the comprehension questions. Mr. Alonzo also plans to collect a measure of Adam's oral fluency rate.

Socially, Adam is holding his own. He misses some classroom instruction because he goes to work with Mr. Alonzo, but he manages to maintain his friendships with peers. Ms. Riley notices that he is prone to some outbursts in class, especially during science instruction. He also continues to wander during independent reading time. After 16 weeks of Tier 2 supplemental intervention, Adam has not progressed far, and he and the classroom teacher meet again with Adam's parents. They all agree that he is not making the progress they had hoped for, and Mr. Alonzo's data collection on fluency, comprehension, and decoding bears this out. Adam's mom and dad agree that a Tier 3 intensive intervention, also implemented by Mr. Alonzo, might help. This involves the use of a phonics-based intervention program purchased by the district specifically for this level of support. As part of this process, Adam meets with Mr. Alonzo for 30 minutes every day.

Mr. Alonzo likes the intervention program because it works through a series of prescribed lessons, each accompanied by an online assessment tool that allows the teacher to chart results over time. The visual representations are a clear way to evaluate each student's progress. Toward the end of the school year, Adam begins to make some gains (especially in decoding), but his comprehension still lags, preventing him from reading more complex texts. Another meeting is scheduled, this time with the school's Student Study Team. Adam's parents are in attendance, and Ms. Riley begins the meeting by reminding everyone, "Our main job here is to figure out how we can help Adam learn." The team discusses the previous interventions and notes that Adam is not making the desired progress. They decide to refer Adam for special education testing, and Adam's parents consent.

Adam has demonstrated difficulty with the 5th grade curriculum but has made some progress. The results of his testing do not show that he meets eligibility requirements for a federally handicapping condition. His teacher recommends that Adam attend the six-week summer school so he can revisit 5th grade content. He is promoted to 6th grade but one of the 6th grade teachers says, "We're not quite sure what to do next. I guess we'll start fresh and see what happens."

The RTI^2 School: "How Can Focusing on Adam Help the System Improve?"

After meeting the important people in the school (the principal, the custodian, and the lunch staff), Adam settles into his 5th grade class. His teacher, Ms. Riley, is experienced with this age group and has been a staff member at the school for 15 years. Adam likes his new class and soon establishes social relationships with his peers. He is quickly seen as an asset in any recess game and is well liked by other children, who say he is "nice."

The reading block is his least favorite part of the day. His teacher used some simple screening instruments on his first day, including the San Diego Quick, a word list that targets decoding skills, and a cloze assessment on simple machines that was based on a recent chapter from the science textbook. Ms. Riley knows that these screening instruments should not be used as factors in big decisions, but they provide a starting point for making initial instructional decisions. The results of the decoding assessment show that Adam is decoding at about a 3rd grade level. In addition, he struggled to complete the cloze assessment, accurately completing only 36 percent of the words and indicating that he had difficulty comprehending the passage. Ms. Riley wonders whether it was an issue of background knowledge or difficulty with reading comprehension skills, so she asks him about his science class at his former school. "We were learning about plant and animal cells," he reports, which suggests to Ms. Riley that at least part of the problem might be background knowledge.

The following day, Ms. Riley gives Adam another cloze assessment— one that uses a passage on plant cells. He scores higher this time—52 percent—but not as high as she had hoped; he should have been familiar with the content and needed a score of at least 60 percent to be considered at an independent level. Over the next few days, she gathers other information, including the Metacomprehension Strategies Index (MSI) (Schmitt, 1990). She administers this 25-item questionnaire at the beginning of the school year to all of her students so that she can make some initial grouping decisions. Because it is just Adam that she needs to assess, she conducts it as an interview in order to learn some other things about him as well. During the course of administering the MSI, she learns that Adam is friendly and has good oral language skills. He sometimes prefers to chat rather than answer the questions, but he is good-natured about finishing the interview. When Ms. Riley analyzes the results, she learns that her new student is good at self-questioning but has difficulty drawing on his background knowledge and verifying his predictions.

She knows that the next round of benchmark testing will occur in a few weeks, and this will offer a better opportunity to measure Adam's reading ability. However, given that she already sees some early signs of difficulty, she uses the Qualitative Reading Inventory-4 (QRI-4) informal reading inventory to delve deeper (Leslie & Caldwell, 2005). The word list and subsequent passages help her determine that Adam is reading at a

DAZE Assessment for
Comprehension may.
find on OSU website.

late 3rd grade level. During the assessment, Adam has difficulty answering implicit comprehension questions but does better on explicit ones. Ms. Riley appreciates the usefulness of QRI-4, a tool that one of the special educators in the school's RTI[2] work group shared with the 5th grade team.

Ms. Riley places Adam in a reading group with four other children at similar reading levels. Using text matched to their instructional level, Ms. Riley meets three times a week with this guided reading group and always devotes one reading to science content so Adam can catch up on content he missed. There are other groups who read at higher levels; she meets with them only once or twice a week. "I didn't always do that," she says. "I used to think it all had to be 'fair'—you know, equal. At some point I realized that the fairest system is when everyone gets what they need."

In the meantime, the results of the benchmark assessment are clear—Adam is reading well below his peers. Fortunately, the elementary school has invested in a Response to Instruction and Intervention initiative. Ms. Riley consults with Ms. Leung, the speech-language pathologist at the school, and describes her initial findings about Adam. Ms. Leung agrees that Adam might benefit from additional language instruction on asking metacognitive questions. Ms. Leung is in Ms. Riley's classroom once a week to meet with two other students who qualify for language services. After one of her sessions with the students who have identified disabilities, she listens for a few minutes to a guided reading lesson that Ms. Riley leads with Adam and a few others. Based on her observations, Ms. Leung shares a self-inquiry strategy that Ms. Riley begins to use with Adam's group: after previewing the story, give each student in the group a key question on a card:

- What do I already know about this topic?
- Have I read anything else by this author?
- What are two facts or ideas I expect to read about?
- I would be completely surprised if the author discussed _____.

The students answer their questions, and then each adds information to these initial responses. Ms. Riley records this information on her laptop so students can review their answers after they have read the story.

In addition, during one lunch hour a week, Adam meets with a book club hosted by the school's reading specialist. Called the Lunch Bunch, students in 4th through 6th grade who are experiencing reading difficulties due to motivation and interest are invited to participate in this club. Adam reads items of his choosing from a list developed by the reading specialist.

Adam likes professional wrestling magazines. He talks with other students who are reading the same magazine, and the reading specialist listens in on the conversation and brokers discussions about *lucha libre* (a style of wrestling) in general and Rey Mysterio (a popular wrestler) in particular.

Adam also participates in more formal Tier 2 supplemental reading instruction. The Title I teacher, Mr. Alonzo, works in Ms. Riley's classroom once a week during the reading block and provides additional small-group instruction for several students. He assessed Adam's phonics knowledge early on and learned that Adam had difficulties with phonics skills. Based on plans developed with Ms. Riley and consultations with the reading specialist and speech pathologist, Mr. Alonzo focuses on developing these skills in conjunction with written summaries of the material that Adam and the others read in class. Using both holistic and analytic measures, including conventions, words written, and the number of words per sentence, Mr. Alonzo collects data on Adam's writing samples every two weeks. Adam also takes part in scaffolded writing instruction activities such as modeled writing, Power Writing, generative sentences, and writing models (Fisher & Frey, 2007b).

After 20 weeks of Tier 2 supplemental instruction, Adam's responsiveness rate still concerns his teachers. Once again, the team meets with Adam's parents to discuss his progress and develop new supports. They examine data on Adam's work and look at comparative data from randomly selected, unidentified classmates. Based on his continued difficulties applying metacognitive strategies and creating summaries, the team agrees that Adam would benefit from Tier 3 intensive intervention support. As part of this process, the reading specialist, Ms. Robertson, will work directly with Adam.

A major principle of the RTI[2] program at Adam's school is that both supplemental and intensive interventions are paired as closely as possible with classroom instruction. Therefore, Ms. Robertson consults with Ms. Riley to discuss the social studies and science content that the class will cover. Ms. Robertson locates readings that align with the content in their textbooks, allowing her to preteach and reteach content that Adam will learn in his classroom. In addition, she uses reading passages on these same topics as a vehicle for reading comprehension instruction, as well as a basis for targeted phonics work. Importantly, a writing component is included in each lesson. Ms. Robertson notices that Adam seems to write more when he uses a laptop computer, so she encourages him to use one in their work together. She also makes a point of sharing this successful accommodation with Ms. Riley, as an analysis of Adam's writing samples shows that he writes longer and more complex summaries on a laptop than he does by hand.

During the 12 weeks of Tier 3 intensive intervention and support, Adam's grades in all subject areas improve. Though he is not at the top of the class, Ms. Riley and Adam's parents are pleased with his solid *B* average. This school has also established a mechanism for analyzing support results and advising next year's teachers. The school's RTI[2] committee meets monthly to look at data for individual students in Tiers 2 and 3. They also compare incidence rates by grade level and discuss possible Tier 1 refinements to core instruction for students who receive intervention services. In fact, many of the instructional practices used with Adam, including assessment instruments, grouping strategies, and leveled readings, are the product of previous work by this committee. Ms. Riley, a member of the team, says, "I have a more solid classroom now than I did five years ago. I've always been a good teacher, but now I'm a more responsive one."

The last two meetings of the year also include designing continued support for students advancing to the next grade level. Because Adam will be entering 6th grade, the committee's grade-level representative and Ms. Riley discuss possible support for Adam. Ms. Riley shares successes (using a laptop, previewing content in advance of the class, receiving extra support to complete longer assignments, and having high-interest independent reading material). The 6th grade team has implemented an academic recovery period once a week so that assignment support is available to any student who needs it. The committee recommends that Adam attend the extended school year program to keep him engaged in reading and writing and to avoid the summer slide during which achievement levels decline from a lack of instruction or engagement (Alexander, Entwisle, & Olson, 2007).

In contrast to traditional summer school, the extended school year program provides extra days for students to master content standards from the regular school year (more information on extended school year programs can be found in Chapter 4). Adam's family agrees that this is a good plan. Adam, who has had a positive experience with his new school, has a good attitude about himself as a learner. "The best thing about this school," he says, "is that they don't let you fail."

Which Adventure Did You Choose?

Figure 1.1 contains a summary and synthesis of the actions taken by the teachers and the school in each of the three possible scenarios. Admittedly, deciding where to place Adam is a rhetorical dilemma. We can't imagine that anyone reading this book would choose the first scenario. However, we do expect many readers to nod their heads in sad recognition of their own personal experiences as educators, parents, or students. In the past, special education prereferral processes were regarded as a foregone conclusion for struggling students. Unfortunately, there has been a long tradition of thinking, "There's something wrong with this kid, and whatever it is, he doesn't belong in my class."

The second scenario is a more enlightened one that is commonly seen in many education communities as states implement RTI plans, and well-meaning teachers and administrators follow guidelines to examine a student's responsiveness to intervention. When the student fails to respond positively, the process for special education testing is initiated. However, we believe that there remains a largely untapped potential to improve this process by capitalizing on the collective wisdom of educators and families, which explores the spirit of the law while operating within its guidelines. We have all witnessed what committed educators and families can accomplish when the artificial barriers set up by strict role definitions are intentionally blurred. Response to Instruction and Intervention seeks to expand the lens so that both the classroom and individual students benefit from this collaboration. To this end, we intend this book to serve the following purposes:

- Define *Response to Intervention*.
- Examine a model that integrates instruction and intervention (RTI^2).
- Clarify misconceptions about RTI^2.
- Extend the RTI^2 approach across subject areas and grade levels.
- Offer best practices and practical considerations regarding the implementation of RTI^2.
- Discuss how to strengthen school improvement efforts using RTI^2.

Figure 1.1

A Comparison of the Interventions and Supports in the Three Scenarios

The Traditional School *What's wrong with Adam?*	The RTI School *How can we help Adam?*	The RTI² School *How can focusing on Adam help the system improve?*
Behavioral referrals	Informal classroom assessments	Informal classroom assessments
Benchmark assessments	Student conference	Student conference
Remedial reading group with paraprofessional	Benchmark assessments	Instructional plan developed by classroom teacher
Parent conferences	Tier 2 intervention, assessment, and progress monitoring	More informal classroom assessments
Learning contract	Parent meetings	Differentiated reading groups with increased time
Intersession attendance	Commercial Tier 3 intervention program, assessment, and progress monitoring	Benchmark assessments
Teacher meetings	Student Study Team with parents	Consultation with special educator
Student Study Team	Special education testing	Lunch Bunch book club
Special education testing	Summer school	Tier 2 intervention with consultation (special educator, Title I teacher, reading specialist, and classroom teacher)
Summer school		Parent meetings
		Individual instruction
		Tier 3 intervention aligned to classroom instruction
		Tier 3 feedback loop to classroom teacher
		RTI² committee to examine school improvement
		Grade level meetings to design continued support for the following year

The Takeaway

At the end of each chapter, we will reiterate key points in a feature we call "The Takeaway." This short bulleted list is meant to be both a summary and a means for you to check your own understanding of the information we have presented. In this chapter, we addressed the following ideas:

• Earlier iterations of the prereferral process were often seen as a necessary formality that almost always led to special education testing.

• Response to Intervention (RTI) plans shift the focus to examine interventions that might prevent referral for testing.

• Response to Instruction and Intervention (RTI^2) plans seek to capitalize on the RTI approach as a means of continually examining classroom instructional design. Consultation and collaboration with other professionals and families is essential.

2

Response to Intervention:
Defining and Refining the Process

Pick up any education journal, scan any conference program, or even eavesdrop on a conversation between educators, and you're likely to see or hear RTI mentioned. When we typed "response to intervention" into the Google search engine in October 2009, we got 22,800,000 hits. In what has become a defining cultural marker of this decade, there are "response to intervention" entries on both Wikipedia and Facebook.

RTI is currently a hot topic in the education field, but, like any "new" idea, it has its critics and advocates. While we are intrigued with the notion that one can become a "fan" of RTI on Facebook, the concept has significant, real-world implications for students, families, teachers, and administrators. In this chapter, we'll define RTI, explore its historical roots, and consider the effectiveness of this approach in improving student achievement. First, let's explore the issue that RTI was designed to address.

What Is Response to Intervention?

In many schools, instruction and time are constant—they do not vary on a student-by-student basis. RTI was designed as a way to encourage teachers to vary instruction and time to create a constant level of learning. A core assumption of RTI is that all students can reach high levels of achievement if the system is willing (and able) to vary the amount of time students have to learn and the type of instruction they receive. Thus, RTI builds on work done with differentiated instruction (Tomlinson, 2001) and understanding by design (Wiggins & McTighe, 2005). See Figure 2.1 for a visual representation of a system in which educational outcomes vary versus a system in which time and instructional interventions vary.

Figure 2.1
Perspectives on Learning

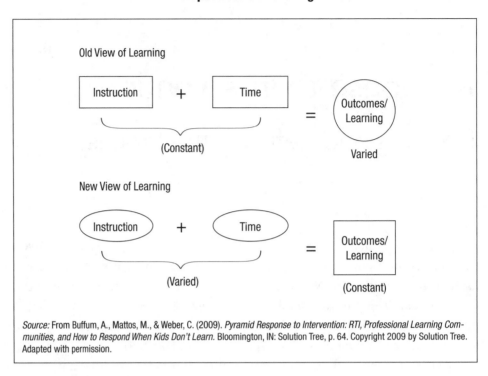

Source: From Buffum, A., Mattos, M., & Weber, C. (2009). *Pyramid Response to Intervention: RTI, Professional Learning Communities, and How to Respond When Kids Don't Learn.* Bloomington, IN: Solution Tree, p. 64. Copyright 2009 by Solution Tree. Adapted with permission.

Response to Intervention, as referenced in the Individuals with Disabilities Education Improvement Act of 2004 (IDEIA), was conceived as a method to ensure that students receive early intervention and assistance before falling too far behind their peers. It requires that these students receive supplementary support, guided by regularly gathered assessment data, referred to as progress monitoring. RTI, as it has come to be known, replaces the prereferral process that occurred before students were recommended for special education testing by the Student Study Team. The prereferral process was seen as problematic because it was not timely or particularly helpful. By the time a case made it to the Student Study Team, the teacher and student were already in crisis, and the team usually didn't offer any guidance that moved beyond stopgap solutions (Gersten & Dimino, 2006).

A long-standing criticism of special education testing and eligibility is that the traditional method for identifying a learning disability, referred to as a discrepancy model, requires the presence of a statistically significant gap between expected and actual performance (Meyer, 2000). Under this model, educators and families were frustrated that students didn't receive more specialized support from the beginning of their difficulties; instead, this support was sometimes delayed several years. Accordingly, the Office of Special Education and Rehabilitation Services states, "The IQ discrepancy criterion is potentially harmful to students as it results in delaying intervention until the student's achievement is sufficiently low so that the discrepancy is achieved" (U.S. Department of Education, 2005). In addition, this "waiting-to-fail" model was widely viewed as damaging to learners who might acquire a negative view of themselves and of learning in general. The so-called "gift of time"—waiting to see if the problem resolved itself—all too often resulted in students who didn't like school or themselves.

Early-intervention researchers were also vocal about the lack of any mechanism to target services for students before the gap grew too wide. The effectiveness of early intervention to prevent later difficulties has been well documented (e.g., Leslie & Allen, 1999; Vellutino & Scanlon, 2001), but it does require a commitment to personnel, professional development, and progress monitoring in order to be effective. Therefore, a major intent of the response to intervention clause in IDEIA was to provide both a mechanism and a motivation for identifying and supporting students who were beginning to fall behind their classmates. Two key factors in this approach are recognizing how well students respond to supplemental support and interventions and collecting data regularly so that educators can make thoughtful decisions about how to refine this support.

How Are Educational Needs and High Cholesterol Alike?

The RTI model should be familiar to you, as it is commonly used in other fields. For example, the concept of looking closely at a subject's response to treatment—or lack thereof—has deep roots in the medical profession. A classic way to evaluate the effectiveness and benefit of a treatment is to monitor the patient's reaction to it. Let's say that you visit your physician and are found to have elevated cholesterol levels. Your physician might prescribe several treatments at once: change your diet, lose 20 pounds, walk 30 minutes every day, and take a statin medication. Neither you nor your doctor is particularly concerned about which treatment has the highest impact, as long as the net effect of all the treatments is a lower cholesterol count. Your doctor monitors your progress with regularly scheduled measures (i.e., blood tests) to determine whether the treatments are having the desired effect. The extent to which you respond to this treatment influences the doctor's decisions about altering the intensity, duration, or frequency of the treatment. If the desired effect isn't realized, your doctor might ask you to walk for an hour a day, cut back further on some high-cholesterol foods, or increase your medication dosage. If your cholesterol levels show a resistance to these treatments, the doctor might resort to drawing on the expertise of others and refer you to a lipid specialist to examine underlying metabolic causes for high cholesterol.

It is important to note that physicians recommend a course of treatment (diet, weight loss, exercise, and medication) because of clinical trials that examine the effectiveness of each approach. Those clinical trials have a rigorous research design; drug companies study only one variable at a time, use treatment and control groups, and in some cases apply and then withdraw a treatment to see if the effects are reversed. This is a single-subject A-B-A-B research design, where A signifies the baseline condition (without medication) and B signifies the treatment (with medication). One way to examine effectiveness is to see if conditions return to baseline when treatment is withheld. Negative changes in the graph would therefore demonstrate effectiveness of the treatment.

Most classroom applications don't need to rely on a single-subject A-B-A-B research design. As a teacher, you are more like the physician than the drug company scientist. You're looking for the net effect—in other words, are we making progress? To what extent are we making progress? You might also ask yourself, "Do I need to redouble my efforts in one or more areas to alter the rate of progress?" You do not systematically offer and withdraw treatment to see the effect but rather determine if the combination of instruction and intervention is proving effective.

Classroom practices tend to rely on designs that target the net effect, much like those employed by your physician. An important variable that the classroom teacher can manipulate is *intensity*. For instance, Barnett and colleagues (2004) describe the intervention plan for Abby, a 2nd grade student who was falling behind her peers. In the first phase (A), Abby's teacher assessed her oral reading fluency and compared it with five peers, noting that Abby's performance was well below theirs. The first treatment phase (B) consisted of workbook practice. There wasn't much of an increase in Abby's scores, so the teacher introduced a new treatment (C) that involved teacher modeling and reading aloud to peers four days per week. Abby's fluency rate began to increase, but the gap was continuing to widen between her and her peers. Therefore, in the third treatment phase (D), Abby worked on word drills with a reading specialist four days per week. Her rate increased until it was similar to that of her peers, at which point she returned to the second treatment (C) of teacher modeling and reading aloud to peers. However, her peers' fluency rate continued to increase while hers stabilized, so the school's child study team referred her for further special education testing.

Consider the difficulties a student such as Abby might face in a school that does not look at her responsiveness to the first intervention. We'll apply the work of Buffum and colleagues (2009) to Abby's experience. Abby's reading instruction totals 90 minutes each day, and all students in her class experience essentially the same instruction during that time. Therefore, the only component that can vary is her learning—the one element we *don't* want to vary! In this scenario, Abby learns less than her peers and falls further behind the longer she is in school.

However, in a school where responsiveness to intervention is considered, her teacher notices that Abby is failing and designs supplemental instruction to complement the core instruction in her reading block. The teacher designs lessons that meet Abby's learning needs, in addition to more frequent assessments. When Abby does not seem to make gains at a rate that would help to close the gap, she receives more intensive instruction with a reading specialist. Although this scenario results in a referral for special education testing, it should not be seen as a failure. In Abby's school, instruction and time are the variables, differentiated among peers, and learning is held as the constant.

Data-Based Decision Making

One of the foundations of any RTI effort is a system to examine student performance and make instructional decisions based on that information. These data-based decision-making models are typically thought of as a cycle of data collection, analysis and reflection, instructional planning, and intervention (see Figure 2.2).

Data Collection

As we will discuss in greater detail in Chapter 6, the effectiveness of RTI is based in large part on the systematic collection of student performance data. These data include information about instructional context and the strengths and needs of each student. Every child's success is affected by multiple factors, including the teacher's interpretation of standards and related curriculum, possible instructional interventions, materials, and the teacher's self-assessment of additional information that he or she may need to develop and support a successful learning experience for each child.

Figure 2.2
Data-Based Decision-Making Cycle

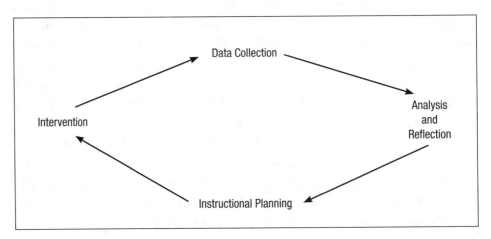

In addition to scrutinizing the environmental context and their own practices, effective teachers use performance data to obtain a thumbnail sketch of each child so that appropriate instruction and interventions can be planned. It is during this phase that teachers should draw on observations, checklists, work samples, interviews, and professional judgment to evaluate the match between the learner and the many factors that influence his or her academic and social growth.

Analysis and Reflection

As we will discuss in Chapter 7, there is a considerable amount of data available to teachers today, and teachers must use these data in their classrooms. Data analysis is critical to instructional planning. Reflecting on what has worked—and on what hasn't—is vitally important if all students are going to develop and learn. Gone are the days when teachers planned a year's worth of lessons in advance. Lesson planning in an RTI system requires continuous data analysis and reflection that guide instructional planning. Although the system may seem foreign to teachers who have each day of their year planned out in advance, it is in fact much more responsive to the individual needs of students.

Instructional Planning

Armed with information about their students' strengths and needs, teachers should plan instruction and interventions based on expectations for the grade level—as expressed in the content and performance standards—and on students' current performance profiles. Teachers can establish an instructional framework that allows for systematic and needs-based teaching, as we will discuss in Chapter 3. The model we propose is based on a gradual release of responsibility as an organizing tool in planning. As part of the instructional planning, teachers group students in a way that will accommodate learning growth as they work with the whole class, independently, and in small homogeneous or heterogeneous configurations. Flexible grouping patterns provide teachers with the structural formats needed to implement and continuously assess a variety of instructional interventions.

Intervention

Appropriate instruction and intervention must acknowledge, celebrate, and support learning differences. Carefully designed, explicit instruction is delivered in a variety of grouping contexts through modeling, prompts, guidance, error correction, practice, and reinforcement. Through interactions with students during instruction and assessment of work samples and behaviors, teachers amass performance data, evaluate their students' needs, and subsequently make modifications to interventions, extensions, and next steps for each student. The ultimate goal is that each child will be able to acquire the targeted information, gain fluency of understanding, generalize beyond the information, and transfer and adapt information and skills to new learning problems and situations.

The cycle then begins again. Using assessment information, teachers analyze and reflect, plan, and deliver new lessons. Along the way, they notice which students have failed to respond to the instruction and thus may need supplemental or intensive interventions. This is RTI in a nutshell: a system designed to ensure that all students reach high levels of achievement.

Is It Effective?

In February 2009, the Institute of Education Sciences, a federally funded initiative responsible for the What Works Clearinghouse, labeled RTI as an effective process for helping students in grades K–2 with early reading difficulties (Gersten, Compton, et al., 2009). The same organization issued similar findings for elementary and middle school mathematics students a few months later (Gersten, Beckman, et al., 2009). The research on using a Response to Intervention approach is promising, although the current knowledge base is disproportionately concentrated in the elementary grades, specifically in the fields of mathematics and reading. In 2002, Baker, Gersten, and Lee performed a meta-analysis of 17 empirically rigorous studies on mathematics interventions for students at risk in grades 2–11. While the individual approaches varied widely, the researchers found that explicit instruction in operations, accompanied by extensive practice and a strong family communication component, resulted in significant positive effects. Similarly, Bryant and colleagues (2008) worked with 1st grade students who were falling behind their classmates in mathematics. A 23-week intervention of 20-minute lessons that focused on number sense and arithmetic yielded positive gains for most of the children involved.

This approach has also produced good results in studies of children with reading difficulties. Among many published studies, a longitudinal study by Simmons and colleagues (2008) of students who participated in reading intervention in kindergarten demonstrated continued positive growth through 3rd grade. This notion of sustained growth is essential to evaluating Response to Intervention efforts. While short-term growth can provide immediate benefits for learners, interventions should have a significant return on investment. It should be evident that looking at long-term sustained results can provide important feedback about the effectiveness of interventions. It should also be evident that any individual student who fails to demonstrate sustained growth necessitates further targeted intervention.

Tiers of Intervention

Although some students are able to recoup lost ground during a single intervention period, others may need repeated periods of increased time, intensity, or access to expertise. The three tiers of intervention (see

Figure 2.3) represent a path to provide increasing levels of intensity in order to prevent academic difficulties.

Tier 1, the core classroom instruction, involves assessing, instructing, and diagnosing learning difficulties. The focus is on providing quality teaching and implementing systems to determine which students respond to this instruction and which students do not.

Tier 2 is a supplementary phase that can occur either in the regular classroom or as an adjunct to the classroom. In this phase, teachers begin to monitor how students respond to the various interventions that are put in place. In Tier 2, students receive instruction in addition to that received in Tier 1, and assessment occurs more frequently in order to gauge responsiveness and plan subsequent interventions.

Figure 2.3
Tiers of Intervention

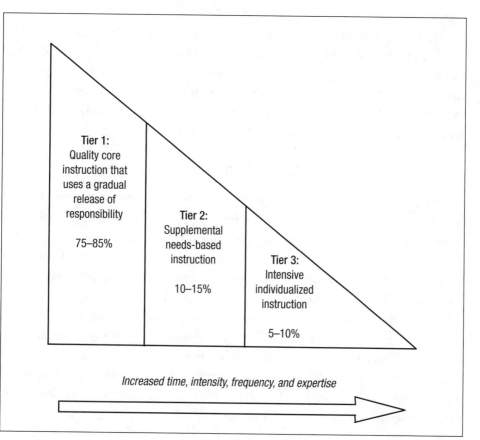

Tier 3 is considered to be an intensive level of intervention. Students in Tier 3 often receive instruction in a one-on-one setting from a curriculum specialist or learning coach. Assessment occurs frequently and may also include diagnostic testing. The following sections examine each tier in more detail.

Tier 1: Core Instruction

The first line of learning is quality core instruction in the classroom. Although often overlooked in the rush to formalize procedures for Tiers 2 and 3, we regard the core instruction of Tier 1 as an essential component of RTI. Tier 1 should include benchmark testing at least three times per school year to gauge student progress—or lack thereof. Another vital component is regularly occurring professional development for teachers to improve and refine their instructional approaches. Approximately 75 to 85 percent of students should make sufficient progress through core instruction alone. Schools where this is not the case should focus on improving core instruction.

Responsive teaching lies at the heart of good instruction, and a gradual release of responsibility model, first described by Pearson and Gallagher in 1983, allows students to take on new learning using scaffolded instruction. Our work during the last decade has focused on refining this model, especially as it relates to the importance of purpose, setting, modeling, and productive group work (e.g., Fisher & Frey, 2008).

Tier 2: Supplemental Intervention

Students who show signs of falling behind their peers need to participate in an additional layer of support—Tier 2, or supplemental intervention. This intervention often takes the form of additional small-group instruction designed to complement the core instruction that all students receive. Student progress is monitored using more frequent assessment and data collection, typically several times per month. It is estimated that 10 to 15 percent of students at one time or another require supplemental interventions in addition to the core instruction. Tier 2 supplemental interventions often last up to 20 weeks so learners can benefit from instruction that focuses on both short- and long-term goals. Keep in mind that these interventions are offered within the general education environment so as to preserve the connection to core curriculum.

Tier 3: Intensive Intervention

There will be students who do not respond positively to the supplemental interventions designed for Tier 2 and will benefit from even more intensive interventions. Five to 10 percent of students will require an intensified approach that includes more time, a lower teacher-student ratio (typically one-to-one), individualized lessons that target weaknesses while leveraging student strengths, and a sophisticated cadre of assessment tools to monitor progress and diagnose difficulties. Tier 3 interventions are also intensified via the involvement of educators who possess expertise about specific academic content. These experts include, but are not limited to, curriculum specialists, coaches, and related service personnel such as speech-language pathologists and intervention specialists.

RTI^2: Preventing "Tears" of Intervention

As noted earlier in this chapter, we advocate for a strengthened model of RTI called Response to Instruction and Intervention (RTI^2). Our experience suggests that educators can't wait to determine if students respond to *intervention*; they have to first determine if students respond to *instruction*. The RTI^2 model has been described by the California Department of Education as

> aligned...curriculum, instruction, and assessment as a coherent system that provides ongoing monthly or weekly data about student progress in core subjects, focuses high quality instruction, and ensures early intervention for students experiencing learning roadblocks [by] pooling knowledge and forming communities of practice around early intervention and effective student support strategies. (2009, §3)

A key principle of RTI^2 is that any intervention is predicated on the notion that Tier 1 core instruction is responsive, standards-based, and data-driven. Best practices require that instruction be scaffolded so that students on all points of the learning continuum can benefit from the educational environment of the general education classroom. RTI^2 is undermined when schools rely on Tier 2 and Tier 3 interventions to compensate for inadequate, unresponsive, and erratic core classroom instruction.

In addition, RTI^2 requires a rich landscape of formative assessments that provide feedback to the learner, including benchmark evaluations for progress monitoring and more precise diagnostic tests to guide effective intervention. This feedback loop also focuses on refining instruction for all students so that the core classroom instruction can be continuously improved.

A third vital component of RTI^2 involves establishing systems that make it possible for educators and families to work together effectively. These "communities of practice" provide a responsive system for early and effective intervention. Although not exclusively a special education initiative, the inclusion of this concept in IDEIA is not coincidental. Special educators and related personnel, general educators, and families should work together in ways that promote collaboration and cooperation. This group effort will yield positive changes in program design and implementation (Frey, 2007).

Establishing an RTI^2 committee is one way to formalize this community of practice. This is a standing work group of general and special educators, administrators, and parent representatives who meet to discuss the progress of individual students and make recommendations concerning intervention and referral for special education testing. However, the work of this committee extends beyond the traditional duties of a Student Study Team. The RTI^2 committee is also charged with examining patterns of teaching and learning at the classroom and grade levels. Other school resources, such as the peer coach or the assessment coordinator, may meet with a group of teachers to refine curricular and instructional approaches. In other cases, a mentor teacher may collaborate with the classroom teacher in a series of tuning sessions that focus on a particular element of learning. Therefore, the RTI^2 committee must work closely with other school improvement groups, including those focused on data analysis and professional development. This feedback loop among work groups increases the ability of each to examine results at the individual, classroom, and grade levels to foster effective practice.

Finally, RTI^2 presumes that some students will require intervention only intermittently. There is a misconception among some educators that *intervention* is just a newer word for *remediation*. In many cases, students who participate in an intervention will gain the necessary knowledge and skills to catch up to their peers and make further support unnecessary. However, it should be anticipated that a few students will need regularly scheduled "doses" of intervention, especially in the primary grades, to keep the gap between them and their peers relatively small. We think of these interventions as academic booster shots. In the same way that booster shots are used to build a child's immune system in order to ward off disease, a series of short-term instructional interventions spread over the first years of school can strengthen a student's academic immune system (Frey, 2003).

Keep in mind that the key to the RTI² model is *responsiveness*, not remediation. Data are used to measure the extent to which an intervention is working. Students can respond to an intervention without closing the entire gap at once. However, a widening gap, as evidenced in a student such as Abby, may warrant further testing. The goal is not to provide a fast track to special education testing but instead to ensure that other possibilities, including ineffective core instruction and a lack of educational experiences, are not responsible.

Asking the Hard Questions

A school or district undertaking RTI² must be willing to ask hard questions about its ability to deliver quality instruction at each tier in the system. The approach also requires a willingness to examine the extent to which core classroom instruction is providing effective programming. The importance of this step cannot be overstated. As noted previously, interventions should not be used to compensate for ineffective classroom instruction. An unresponsive classroom is likely to tax the finite resources, fiscal as well as human, of even the best intervention systems. Therefore, the communities of practice dedicated to developing and improving program design and implementation must prioritize by asking themselves the difficult questions that can ultimately lead to better instruction for all learners. W. David Tilly, Director of Innovation and Accountability at the Heartland Area Education Agency in Iowa and a noted scholar in the Response to Intervention field, advises communities of practice to ask themselves these questions:

1. Is our core program sufficient?
2. If the core program is not sufficient, what led to this?
3. How will the needs identified in the core program be addressed?
4. How will the sufficiency and effectiveness of the core program be monitored over time?

5. Have improvements to the core program been effective?

6. For which students is the core instruction sufficient or insufficient?

7. What specific supplemental and intensive instruction is needed?

8. How will specific supplemental and intensive instruction be delivered?

9. How will the effectiveness of supplemental and intensive instruction be monitored?

10. How will we determine which students need to move to a different level of instruction? (Tilly, 2008)

These questions can guide schools and districts to develop intervention systems that will truly meet the needs of learners. Student responsiveness is only part of the picture. Educators must be willing to ask themselves how responsive the current system is to the needs of students, teachers, and families.

The Takeaway

After reading this chapter, consider the following key points:

• It is imperative that teachers first consider individual students' responses to quality core instruction before recommending supplemental and intensive interventions. They must also determine which students respond to the interventions and continue adapting instructional routines and time to achieve the desired results.

• RTI[2] begins with strong core instruction built on a gradual release of responsibility model.

• RTI[2] relies on a strong assessment component to make intervention decisions, monitor progress, and improve instruction in all tiers.

• RTI[2] emphasizes a collaborative approach to classroom support.

• RTI[2] anticipates that some students will periodically cycle through interventions—an approach we liken to an academic booster shot.

3

Quality Core Instruction:

A Necessary First Step

It should go without saying that all students need access to quality instruction, the first component of an RTI² system. Without high-quality initial instruction, significant numbers of students will require supplemental instruction and intensive intervention that are costly and time-consuming, an approach that is in opposition to a continuous school improvement model. Unfortunately, far too few students have access to a basic foundation of quality instruction. We are all familiar with the following instructional events:

- In a 1st grade class, children independently complete practice pages from a workbook.
- In a 4th grade class, students are assigned a writing prompt and have 30 minutes to respond.
- In an 8th grade class, students are told to read a particular textbook chapter and then answer the questions at the end of the chapter.
- In a 10th grade algebra class, students are given 15 problems and told to work on them quietly in class and finish the problems for homework.

In each of these scenarios, the students are not actively taught; they are effectively made responsible for their own instruction—it's do-it-yourself learning. Interestingly, the students who perform well in these classrooms are those who already understand the content. It's not hard to complete a worksheet (or a "shut-up sheet," as one of our colleagues calls it) when you have already mastered the information. Nor is it hard to answer end-of-chapter questions when you already read at grade level and are familiar with the genre of questions often asked in textbooks.

Clearly, the "busywork" examples we've cited are not exemplars of quality teaching. They rather represent a phenomenon in which teachers *cause* or *assign* work, rather than teach. If all students are to meet the high expectations we hold for them, they need access to high-quality core instruction that enables them to marshal previously learned concepts to reach new understandings.

How might we realize this goal? We can do it with a purposeful, yet gradual, release of responsibility model (see Figure 3.1). This model provides quality core instruction designed to build student competence and independence by providing examples of the thinking required to complete the work. Part of this core instruction involves access to academic language, peer support, and needs-based guided instruction. In this chapter, we'll begin by establishing purpose for our instruction and discuss how the process can be used to promote independent learning. We'll then focus on a series of instructional routines that are integral to quality teaching.

Figure 3.1
Release of Responsibility Model

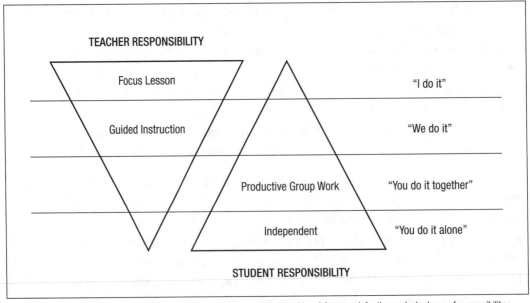

Source: From Fisher, D., & Frey, N. (2008). *Better learning through structured teaching: A framework for the gradual release of responsibility.* Alexandria, VA: ASCD. Adapted with permission.

Establishing Purpose

First and foremost, teachers must establish the purpose of their instruction with students in a clear and coherent manner. Students need to understand the reasons behind a lesson, as well as what they are supposed to do with the information, in order to accurately perform the tasks expected of them. In addition, a coherent purpose makes it possible for learners to access the background knowledge of learned concepts in order to build schema. When teachers clearly establish a purpose and then align instructional events with that purpose, they can determine which students respond to the instruction and which do not. When the purpose is not clear or agreed upon, students may complete a number of tasks yet fail to master the intended content, skills, or strategies. They may also fail to understand the content's relevance or know what they are supposed to do with information. Students are practically begging for an established purpose when they ask, "What do we gotta know?"

An established purpose should address both content and language goals, especially for English language learners (Dong, 2004/2005; Hill & Flynn, 2006), and content goals should come directly from the standards. Figure 3.2 contains sample content and language objectives from an elementary school.

There are a number of ways to determine language objectives, depending on student needs. Language goals will sometimes focus on vocabulary since students of all ages need to attend to both specialized and technical words. Specialized words are those that change meaning in different contexts or content areas, including *process*, *set*, *prime*, and *expression*. Technical words are specific to a discipline and are rarely used elsewhere, such as *rhombus*, *photosynthesis*, and *denominator*. A vocabulary-related language goal related to the study of the moon might be to use the terms *full*, *half*, *quarter*, and *new* to explain the moon's phases.

Alternatively, a language purpose might focus on language structure by invoking grammar, syntax, signal words, or sentence frames. Keeping with the moon example, a structure-related goal might be to use sequence words (*first, next, then, last*) to explain the phases of the moon. Finally, the language goal might be based on the functions of language—to question, summarize, explain, express opinions, justify, inform, persuade, and so on. When studying the moon, a function-related language goal might be to explain how the moon, the sun, and Earth move through the phases.

Figure 3.2
Sample Content and Language Goals

Kindergarten: Language Arts

Content Objective: Identify the characters, setting, and important events after hearing a story.

Language Objective: Retell the story and include characters, setting, and at least three events using a story map.

1st Grade: Math

Content Objective: Determine how many tens and ones are in a set.

Language Objective: Apply the sentence frame "_____ groups of ten and _____ ones equals _____." (e.g., "3 groups of tens and 2 ones equals 32.")

2nd Grade: Life Science

Content Objective: Compare and contrast the life cycles of frogs and butterflies.

Language Objective: Describe similarities and differences between the life cycles of a frog and butterfly.

3rd Grade: Language Arts

Content Objective: Evaluate key features of common texts.

Language Objective: Justify why a passage is categorized as poetry, fiction, or nonfiction.

4th Grade: Earth Science

Content Objective: Recognize how landslides, volcanic eruptions, and earthquakes cause changes to rocks.

Language Objective: Use technical vocabulary to discuss how rocks reflect the processes that formed them.

5th Grade: Social Studies

Content Objective: Analyze one major cause of the American Revolution.

Language Objective: Apply compare/contrast signal words in a written explanation of a major cause of the American Revolution.

6th Grade: Math

Content Objective: Differentiate between relevant and irrelevant information in word problems.

Language Objective: Explain which aspects of a word problem are relevant and irrelevant.

Figure 3.3 provides a summary of the type of language goals useful in planning quality core instruction.

Figure 3.3
Language Goal Types

Category	Type	Definition	Examples
Vocabulary	Specialized	Words whose meanings change depending on context or content	*problem, simplify, value, tissue, vessel*
	Technical	Words that represent one concept only, typically in a specific discipline	*denominator, photosynthesis, concerto, meiosis*
Language Structure	Grammar and syntax	Rules for the use of language	complete sentences, plurals, verb/noun agreement
	Signal words	Guideposts to support listener/reader understanding	*if/then, first, last, compared to*
	Sentence frames	Linguistic scaffolds for apprentice language users that provide some part of a sentence for their use	"On the one hand, _____. But on the other hand, _____."
Language Function	Function	The intent or purpose of the message, which guides construction of the message	to express an opinion, to summarize, to persuade, to question, to entertain, to inform, to sequence, to disagree, to debate, to evaluate, to justify

Across the content areas, language plays a key role in learning. Thus, it is critical to carefully establish a purpose that is related to the linguistic demands of a task. Without such a purpose, students aren't sure what to pay attention to, and they may not respond to the instruction as expected. The result will often be students who require supplemental and/or intensive instruction that could have been addressed at the core instruction level. The first tier of RTI[2]—core instruction—is essential to reduce the need for more intensive interventions.

Teacher Modeling

Teacher modeling is another critical component of releasing responsibility to students. Simply stated, students deserve an example of the thinking and language required by a task before they are asked to engage in the work independently. In addition, there is evidence that humans are hard-wired to mimic or imitate other humans (Winerman, 2005), and this might explain why modeling is so effective. Further, there is evidence that scientists, historians, and mathematicians think differently than other people, and that this style of thinking is part of the discipline in which students need to be apprenticed (Shanahan & Shanahan, 2008).

Modeling requires that teachers provide an example of what happens in their own minds as they solve problems, read, write, or complete tasks. The modeling process does not involve a detailed explanation, nor is it a time to question students; rather, it is an opportunity to demonstrate the ways that experts think. Expert teachers provide excellent models for their students to use. We found that expert teachers focused their modeling in specific areas, including comprehension, word solving, text structures, and text features (Fisher, Frey, & Lapp, 2008). See Figure 3.4 for a self-assessment rubric related to purpose and modeling.

Comprehension

As readers read, they employ a number of cognitive strategies to ensure understanding, such as questioning, inferring, making connections, summarizing, monitoring, predicting, and so on. The key is to know when to use each of these strategies and then to automate that process. For example, predicting isn't always helpful; it's helpful when the author provides specific kinds of information that the reader can use. While reading a specific text, a teacher might share his or her prediction and then ask students to talk with partners about their own predictions. For instance, 9th grade English teacher Ms. Moore pauses during a shared reading of Jesus Colon's short story "Kipling and I" and speculates aloud why the author would describe a gilt-framed poem so early in the story. "This must be an important object to the narrator," she offers. "I'll need to keep reading to find out." Later in the story, she asks herself a question and predicts what the character will do next. Over time, and with significant practice, students will approximate the behaviors they see modeled and reach automaticity with the necessary skills to read complex texts on their own.

Figure 3.4

Quality Indicators for Purpose and Modeling

Indicators	4: Exemplary	3: Proficient	2: Approaching	1: Minimal
Purpose is established for both content and language outcomes and is based on formative assessments.	Purpose is explicitly presented through content and language goals, which are based on content standards and the language demands of the task, as well as students' needs identified via formative assessments.	Language and content goals are stated but not well connected to content standards or the language demands of the task. Goals address students' needs identified via formative assessments.	Only one purpose is stated (i.e., either the content purpose or the language purpose is missing), or the purpose is not well connected with content standards; the language demands of the task, or students' needs as identified via formative assessments.	No content or language outcomes are stated or implied. Purpose is implied but not stated, and there is no evidence of the use of formative assessments to plan instruction.
The essential lesson elements of guided, collaborative, and independent tasks accurately reflect the established purpose.	All tasks that students actually complete throughout the lesson reflect the content and language purposes.	Most tasks that students actually complete throughout the lesson reflect the content and language purposes.	Some tasks that students actually complete throughout the lesson reflect the content and language purposes.	The tasks that students complete during the lesson are not consistent with the stated purposes.
Students can explain the purpose in their own words.	Randomly selected students can explain or demonstrate how the stated purposes relate to their own learning.	Students can accurately restate the purpose of the lesson but lack a clear understanding of why they are taught the content.	Students can restate portions of the purpose of the lesson but lack an understanding of why they are taught the content.	Students are unable to correctly state the purpose of the lesson.
Teacher provides an authentic model.	Modeling includes naming the task or strategy and explaining when it is used. The teacher alerts learners about errors to avoid and shows them how the strategy is applied to check for accuracy. Modeling consistently contains "I" statements.	Modeling contains all the indicators (naming, explaining, analogies, demonstration, errors to avoid, and checking), but the teacher only uses some "I" statements.	Modeling contains some indicators (e.g., naming and explaining), but the teacher directs students through the use of "you" statements.	Modeling contains few indicators. The teacher uses "you" statements that focus on directions and process, not modeling of thinking.
Students use strategies and skills that were modeled.	After receiving adequate time in scaffolded instructional support, all students can complete tasks using the strategy or skill that was modeled.	After receiving limited time in scaffolded instructional support, students complete tasks using the strategy or skill that was modeled.	Students move directly from teacher modeling to independent work, with little to no scaffolded instructional support.	There is a mismatch between what was modeled and what students are asked to do.

Word Solving

Given the demands of vocabulary learning in school and the impact that word knowledge has on understanding, it is clear that teachers should model word solving. Rather than tell students the meaning of unfamiliar words as they are encountered, expert teachers model the ways in which unknown words are discovered. Readers sometimes solve unknown words by using context clues; we call this an "outside-the-word" strategy. For example, a teacher might pause on an unfamiliar word and model, solving it with an illustration and surrounding words. Of course, context clues are not always useful. In addition to helpful clues, readers may encounter nondirective and misdirective clues.

When context clues are not helpful, proficient readers look "inside" the word for meaning, using prefixes, suffixes, bases, roots, cognates, or word families to help determine meaning. Teacher modeling of this strategy provides students with transferable skills they can use when they encounter unknown words. For example, while reading a science text, Mr. Bonine stops at the word *carnivore* and models his thinking about the Spanish word *carne* (meaning "meat"), which he says helps him remember that carnivores are meat eaters. When context clues and word parts are not helpful, teachers model the use of resources such as dictionaries, Web sites, and knowledgeable peers. As with comprehension, word solving is a skill that must be taught, developed, and automated if students are to assume responsibility for their learning.

Text Structures

One of the ways that readers make meaning of texts is through an understanding of text structures. Narrative texts use a story grammar that includes characters, setting, plot, conflict, resolution, literary devices, and dialogue. Teachers model their understanding of this grammar as a tool they use to understand the text. For example, Mr. Goodwin pauses during his reading of *The Outsiders* to discuss the themes of loss and redemption revealed when a character recites the Robert Frost poem "Nothing Gold Can Stay." Informational texts also have internal structures, such as problem/solution, cause/effect, compare/contrast, temporal/sequence, and descriptive. The analysis of an informational text's structure allows readers to predict what the author might explain next. It also helps readers remember what they read and organize their thinking about a text. For example, while thinking aloud about a reading on the construction of the Transcontinental Railroad, Ms. Allen notes that the author introduces the problem of pay differences between Chinese and white workers. She says to her students, "Now here's a problem. I can predict that the solution to the problem will come next. That's how authors like to write—with a problem followed by a solution. I can take some notes using a problem and solution chart. Looking at the chart, I remember that in many cases, the solution to one problem creates new, often unexpected, problems. I wonder if that will be the case here?" When she reads the next section, she points out that the author describes the solution reached after the Chinese workers led a strike for higher wages.

Text Features

Finally, students often need assistance understanding and using the text features that are included with many of the texts they read. Text features include tables, charts, figures, illustrations, captions, bold and italicized words, headings, and other extratextual additions to the page. Many students aren't sure when they should read the text features—before, during, or after reading the text?

Through teacher modeling, students can experience the thoughtful analysis of text features, including how to extract the information they need when they need it. Given that so much information can be presented in various text features, it seems reasonable to suggest that most students need instruction that moves them from novice to expert in this regard. Looking at a table on the use of distance as a function of time, as found in a high school math textbook, Ms. Burow reads aloud the column and row headings and notes how to find information accordingly. (Figure 3.5 contains a list of common strategies that math teachers model as part of their instruction.) Ms. Johnson, examining a figure on a map in a 9th grade geography textbook, models the use of a map legend to find the latitude and longitude of a city. Ms. Daily models reading the captions on photographs that accompany a 4th grade science selection on the importance of honeybees for crop pollination.

Teacher modeling is a critical component of quality core instruction. It provides the apprenticeship that learners need in order to apply what they witness to novel tasks. Students who do not have access to appropriate teacher modeling are at risk of thinking and talking at a much more superficial level than is expected for their respective grade level. This is especially true as it relates to monitoring understanding. Without solid examples of how a teacher notices when he or she has lost meaning, and what the teacher does to regain it, students will often simply skip what they don't understand. This practice places students at risk for academic failure and in need of supplemental or intensive intervention.

Figure 3.5
Common Aspects of Math Modeling

Cognitive Strategy	Definition	Example
Background knowledge	Activating knowledge that is already stored in the mind for use with the current problem	"When I see a triangle, I remember that the angles add up to 180°."
Relevant versus irrelevant information	Noticing that there is often more information than is required to solve a problem	"I've read this problem twice, and I know that there is information included that I don't need."
Selecting a function	Reviewing the range of mathematics functions and selecting an appropriate one based on the information provided	"This problem says 'increased by' so I know that I'll have to add."
Setting up the problem	Moving from the words in a problem to an equation that can be solved	"The first thing that I will do is … because …."
Estimating answers	Making an educated guess about the answer, based on the information provided	"I predict that the product will be about 150 because I see that the number is multiplied 10 times."
Determining reasonableness of an answer	Assessing an answer to determine if it is possible, based on the information contained in the problem	"The problem has two numbers in the hundreds, so I know that the answer has to be over 200, but it can't be over 1,000."

Guided Instruction

Establishing purpose and modeling learning behavior is a great start for teachers whose students are beginning to assume responsibility for their learning, but learners also require guided instruction to be successful. We define guided instruction as the strategic use of cues, prompts, and questions designed to facilitate student thinking. Guided instruction should be based on assessment information. While guided instruction can be done with the whole class, our experience suggests that it is most effective with small groups. While other students are engaged in collaborative tasks, the teacher can meet with a small group for guided instruction. Members of this group should be selected based on formative assessment data. In the following discussion, Ms. Grant works with a group of students who misunderstood photosynthesis, and she uses a series of questions and prompts to increase understanding.

Ms. Grant: Some of you thought that plants ate soil to grow. This is a very common misconception that we should talk about further. Do you remember the video we saw about photosynthesis? What role did soil play in that video?

Destini: Well, it wasn't about the dirt. It was about the sun and carbon dioxide.

Andrew: And how the plants make oxygen for humans.

Ms. Grant: Plants make oxygen for humans?

Andrew: Yeah. Well, I guess that they'd make oxygen even if there weren't humans.

Michael: It's called a by-product. They don't make oxygen for humans. They just make oxygen.

Ms. Grant: And what is left, once they've made this oxygen?

Destini: Carbon. They take in carbon dioxide and then give off oxygen, so carbon is left.

Ms. Grant: And what do you know about carbon?

Guided instruction provides teachers with an opportunity to engage students in thinking without explicitly telling them what to think. It's also an opportunity to scaffold student understanding before they're asked to complete tasks independently. In other words, it's a critical component of quality core instruction. The absence of guided instruction necessitates supplemental instruction. When guided instruction is part of the quality core instruction that students receive, many of their learning needs are met as a matter of course.

Productive Group Work

In addition to establishing purpose, modeling, and guided instruction, quality core instruction requires that time is devoted to productive group work. Armed with a clear purpose and a concrete example, students are ready to work—but not yet independently. First, they need time to collaboratively use information in productive ways with their peers. This phase of learning transfers more responsibility to students yet provides them with peer support to be successful. As students interact with one another and with the content, they consolidate their understanding (Frey, Fisher, & Everlove, 2009). When students are prevented from consolidating their understanding, they rapidly forget what they learn and have a difficult time applying knowledge in new situations. The ability to clarify, ask and answer questions, discuss, and reflect is critical throughout their school careers. When students remain isolated from one another, they don't have the opportunity to build these habits of mind. Thus, a lack of access to productive group work can also place students at risk for academic failure and in need of supplemental, intensive instruction.

Regardless of the subject matter or content area, students learn more and retain information longer when they work in productive groups (Beckman, 1990; Totten, Sills, Digby, & Russ, 1991). Students who work in groups also appear more satisfied with their classes, complete more assignments, and generally like school better (Summers, 2006). Groups need interaction, firm deadlines, agreed-upon roles, and interdependent tasks to complete. Collaborative learning tasks are those that could not have been accomplished by an individual; they need to be tasks that require interaction and the natural give-and-take of learning.

The key to collaborative groups lies in accountability; each student must be accountable for some aspect of the collaborative learning task. Unfortunately, this is not always the case. Most teachers can recall group work in which one student did all of the work yet everyone received credit. Not only does this situation prevent some students from learning, but it also thwarts teachers' attempts to check for understanding and link instruction with formative assessments. In addition to individual responsibilities, groups should have accountability for completing tasks. These tasks can vary from something as simple as returning a DVD to its case after viewing to something as complex as writing a group summary of the information learned during the lesson.

In her geometry class, Ms. Chen has students—working in groups of four—complete a collaborative poster for each mathematical proof they solve. Each student is assigned a different-colored marker to use for his or her contribution, and all group members sign their names to their poster. In addition to this collaborative task, the group must ensure that each of its members can explain the proof independently. In other words, students are assuming responsibility for both their and their peers' learning. This approach requires a significant amount of reteaching, negotiation, support, and trust, but the benefits are worth the extra effort.

Independent Learning

Independent learning, such as the application of information to a new situation, is the goal of schooling. Unfortunately, even a cursory look inside a typical classroom reveals that students are often prematurely asked to assume full responsibility for learning in the instructional cycle. As the MetLife survey of homework (Markow, Kim, & Liebman, 2007) revealed, homework is viewed as "important" or "very important" by teachers (83 percent), parents (81 percent), and students (77 percent). However, 26 percent of secondary teachers confessed that they "very often" or "often" assign homework because they run out of time in class. The likelihood of a student successfully completing unfamiliar tasks alone, away from the company of fellow learners or the teacher, is slim.

Newly (or barely) learned tasks do not make for good independent learning. Instead, they require the clearly established purposes, teacher modeling, productive group work, and guided support found in sound classroom instruction. Independent work should be reserved for review and reinforcement of previously taught concepts and applications. This phase of the instructional framework is ideal for the spiral review that so many educators know their students need but rarely get to implement. In addition, it is essential for building connections between previously learned and new concepts. For example, an independent learning task to review the phases of the moon taught earlier in the school year could coincide with new learning about the movement of planets around the sun. Thus, the independent learning task not only provides reinforcement of the moon's phases, but it also deepens understanding of the patterns of movement in the sky and the ways in which the two phenomena influence each another.

Finally, well-structured independent learning tasks should build confidence. By the time a student has reached this phase, he or she should feel prepared for the task. After all, the purpose is clear, and the teacher has modeled how it is done. There has been time for collaborative work with peers, and any necessary guided instruction has been provided. The learner should be at the level of a competent novice, and the purpose is now to refine the existing knowledge and become more expert. After all, isn't this how many of us learned to be teachers?

Independent learning then becomes the ultimate way to build self-esteem through competence. Self-efficacious learners are motivated to take on new concepts because they know that they have been successful in the past and can do it again. Confident learners are more likely to complete homework tasks because they know they can complete them successfully. Too often, students have not had the modeling, guided instruction, and productive group work necessary to be successful independently. However, when they have completed this instructional cycle, learning comes more easily and is also more fun.

Response to Instruction

As you have no doubt surmised, there are many instructional reasons for why students end up needing supplemental and intensive intervention. Failure to implement any aspect of a quality instructional model places students at risk, even students who weren't previously in danger. These students are known as "curriculum casualties" because they fail to learn as a direct result of the poor instruction they receive. A troubling misapplication of RTI is that Tier 2 supplemental support is often used to mitigate ineffective core instruction. As we noted in Chapter 1, the majority of struggling students are performing at lower levels because of experiential or instructional inadequacies, not cognitive ones (Vellutino, Scanlon, Small, & Fanuele, 2006).

In light of this, we are reminded of a student we met when she was in 4th grade. Her experience in school was limited to whole-class instruction and practice sheets. She was delightful to talk to, but she had a very difficult time working with others and read below grade level. There were a number of report cards in her cumulative folder confirming the fact that she had been "slightly below grade level" since 1st grade. However, she was promoted each year without any noticeable improvement or access to supplemental instruction. When she finally had access to quality core instruction, her achievement gap closed, and by 6th grade she was performing on grade level.

Teaching with each of these components is necessary but not sufficient to ensure that an increasing number of students experience success as a result of high-quality core instruction. Teachers must also notice how students respond to instruction and make changes accordingly. While some of those changes will involve supplemental and intensive instruction, alternatives include reteaching a skill or lesson to the whole class, additional guided instruction, or additional opportunities for practice with peers during productive group work.

On the second day of school, David told his teacher that he didn't read books but sometimes read comics (and that his favorite superhero is Daredevil). His teacher wasn't surprised by this information, as David and Daredevil had something in common: a fairly significant vision-related disability. Reduced visual acuity, though, should not necessarily result in poor academic performance. Sadly, David read well below grade level and had struggled for years in school in another county. David's teacher hypothesized that David hadn't had much access to quality core instruction that would have built his competence and confidence.

David was lucky. His new teachers were masters at observing how students respond to instruction and using that information to plan their lessons. For example, David's English teacher found books that David could and would read. David reported that the first book he ever read was *Diary of a Wimpy Kid*, because his teacher talked with him about it as he read and because it was like the comics that he loved so much. In his words, "I never read a whole book before because I don't understand them."

In addition, David responded very positively to the teacher modeling, especially word solving. During guided instruction, David regularly attempted word-solving strategies that his teacher modeled for him. When asked, David said, "I didn't know how to figure out the words before. I just skipped 'em and then quit 'cuz I didn't know what I was reading." The work he produced with his peers was used to plan additional instruction. For example, in his summary of a group task, David spelled *might* as "mite" and *right* as "rite." The obvious lack of understanding of this spelling pattern prompted his teacher to respond with additional lessons.

At the end of the year, David and his English teacher were texting each other. Here is a verbatim transcript of their exchange:

David: U there
Teacher: Yep
David: Were you at sir
Teacher: At a meeting in the district office.

David: I got my report. Those gradez are the best ive ever seen that were min lol

Teacher: Are you proud?? Will you do it again??

David: Yes im proud and I will do it again and these are going to get better.

Teacher: I would LOVE that.

David: But talk to u later sir im going to clean my gmas house and wash my clothes

Teacher: Ok, bye.

In the pages that follow, we provide a sample lesson from a history teacher. As you'll see, the lesson is designed to ensure that students develop an understanding of the content. The vast majority of students will respond favorably to this type of instruction. When the core instruction is of high quality, most students do not need supplemental services or intensive intervention.

A final compelling reason to use a gradual release of responsibility model is that it affords educators a responsive instructional design that makes supplemental and intensive levels of intervention possible. Despite decades of evidence pointing to the effectiveness of differentiated guided and collaborative learning experiences, classrooms are still dominated by teacher-directed whole-class lectures and excessive amounts of independent work. This is true even in elementary classrooms, often thought of as models of this type of responsive instruction. Robert Pianta and his colleagues examined more than 1,000 5th grade classrooms around the country and discovered that 91.2 percent of instructional time was devoted to whole-class instruction and independent work. Further, they noted that findings in 1st and 3rd grade classrooms were similar (Pianta, Belsky, Houts, & Morrison, 2007).

The overuse of lectures and independent work further complicates the ability to design supplemental and intensive interventions in the classroom, in large part because the presence of another adult in the room is seen as an intrusion. Further, the necessary small-group or individual teaching that is needed in intervention work is perceived as vastly different from what other students experience. In short, it's not just students who need to be responsive to intervention; the instructional design of the classroom must be responsive as well.

The following lesson, seen in Figure 3.6, is an excellent example of how solid core instruction that employs a gradual release framework can successfully address a range of learners without producing the "curriculum casualties" that occur when instruction lacks the scaffolding associated with an effective learning design. The lesson begins with modeling a reading selection on the history of immigration in the United States; the teacher thinks aloud about the metacognitive strategies needed to make meaning of the text. The lesson continues with guided instruction for the whole group as they first summarize the reading and then ask questions aloud about immigration. The teacher continues with guided instruction and reviews a document analysis worksheet that the class has used before. The class then divides into four guided instructional groups, and each group analyzes a different set of documents. The teacher moves among these groups, offering further scaffolded instruction to each. After completing the task, members of each guided instruction group reconvene in mixed-ability collaborative groups so they can further their learning with peers who have had different instructional tasks. Finally, the students move to an independent writing assignment using a writing model—an "I Am" poem that scaffolds their learning experience through the use of a partially completed poetic framework (Fisher & Frey, 2007b).

Quality Indicators

Consider the quality indicators present in each phase of the immigration lesson as itemized below.

Establishing Purpose

- Content, language, and social goals are clearly stated.
- Content goal(s) represent grade-level standards and expectations.
- Language goal(s) are focused on oral and written language.
- Students can explain the goals in their own words.

Teacher Modeling

- The content is engaging and provokes thoughtful responses from students.
- The task to be modeled is directly related to later phases of the lesson and to the established purpose.

Figure 3.6

Lesson Plan: Immigration and the Immigrant Experience

Topic/Theme	Standards	Essential Questions	Literacy Connections
Immigration and the immigrant experience	Chronological & Spatial Thinking 1: Students explain how major events are related to one another in time. • 8.12: Students analyze the transformation of the American economy and the changing social and political conditions in the United States in response to the Industrial Revolution.	• How have immigrants contributed to the United States economy? • How are immigrants' experiences similar?	Content Goal: Understand that immigration in the United States is long-standing and complicated. Language Goal: 1. Interpret a written report (secondary source). 2. Interpret images (photographs). 3. Practice writing a conversation. 4. Complete an "I Am" poem. Social Goal: Participate equitably and show openness to other points of view.

Focus Lesson/Direct Instruction/Modeling

• The instructor reads aloud an overview from the Ellis Island Web site titled "The Peopling of America." All students follow along with their own copies. The instructor reads the brief selection twice: the first reading is done straight through to get the overall idea, and the second reading focuses on making the instructor's quest for understanding and question-asking process transparent.

• The instructor displays the resources each group will receive. All students understand the general objective for the day's work before they are assigned their particular documents.

• The instructor models metacognition strategies while reading the brief selection. Included in this think-aloud exercise, the instructor wonders what documents he or she would like to examine to build a better understanding of the immigrant experience. The instructor wonders aloud if the experience was the same for Europeans coming through Ellis Island, Asian immigrants arriving on the West Coast, and Latin American immigrants entering from the southern borders of California, Arizona, and Texas.

• The instructor reconnects with a previously used document analysis worksheet.

Guided Instruction

Whole Group (1)	Whole Group (2)	Small Group (below grade level)	Small Group (at grade level)	Small Group (at grade level and above)	Small Group (proficient and advanced)
• The instructor will review the document analysis worksheet (for purposes of this lesson, the students have experience with this tool). • The instructor will explain two main aspects of interpretation: observation and speculation/interpretation.	Students recall an experience they have had, either positive or negative, with immigrants or immigration. The class questions aloud: *Has immigration in the United States had an overall positive or negative effect?*	Students evaluate two pictures: immigrants landing at Ellis Island and immigrants landing at Angel Island. 1. Students complete a document analysis worksheet for each picture. 2. Students discuss similarities and differences they see in each picture. 3. Students write a paragraph on the back of the worksheet reflecting on the question: *Based upon these two pictures, are the people prepared to work?* Each group member is responsible for reporting aloud to a collaborative group.	Students evaluate two documents: "Brief on Appeal" and "Angel Island Poem #32." 1. Students complete a document analysis worksheet for each document. 2. Students highlight and discuss any words they find in the documents they believe are "loaded" or point to the author having a slanted or predisposed view of the situation represented by the document. 3. Students chart (on an overhead transparency) five specific words they discuss and present their ideas to the class.	• Students examine two documents: "Mexican workers await legal employment in the United States, Mexicali (Mexico)" and a Library of Congress article about Mexican immigration. • Instructor performs an error analysis as needed with learners based on difficulties demonstrated while reading the textbook and secondary sources. 1. Using a highlighter, students identify unfamiliar words and each main idea they come across. 2. Using a pen or pencil, students number the ideas in order. (How does the author use one sentence or idea as a basis for the next point?) 3. With a partner, students write a conversation that they can refer to later ("silent conversation").	• Students receive copies of "Children at Work" and an illustration from the textbook. • Instructor performs a misconception analysis based on previous use of the document analysis worksheet. 1. The instructor walks students through the textbook example with the document analysis worksheet. 2. Students use a clean document analysis worksheet to analyze the picture of children at work. 3. Students complete an "I Am" poem.

Figure 3.6—(continued)

Lesson Plan: Immigration and the Immigrant Experience

Productive Group Work

Collaboration 1	Collaboration 2	Collaboration 3	Collaboration 4
One member from each of the above groups explains one point about the assigned documents. Together, students complete the following sentence: *Immigrants enter the United States with the expectation that*	One member from each of the above groups explains one point about the assigned documents. Students create a thesis statement that justifies immigration from an immigrant's point of view. (i.e., What were the "pull factors" for immigrants?)	One member from each of the above groups explains one point about the assigned documents. Students agree on one major point to complete the following sentence: *One reason people come to the United States is*	One member from each of the above groups explains one point about the assigned documents. Students create a thesis statement that reflects a valid point of view from an immigrant official denying entry to a potential immigrant on the West Coast.

Independent Practice with Conferring

Practice Task(s)	Student/Teacher Conferring
• Students follow writing-to-learn prompts, such as a "silent conversation" or an "I Am" poem. • Students complete Cornell notes as they read the textbook selection on immigration in the United States.	Teachers meet with students to help them form a supporting sentence using a sentence frame.

Assessment

Formative	Summative
• Writing-to-learn prompts (exit tickets) • Short essay explaining the benefits and challenges of immigration	Short essay identifying the benefits of immigration during the late 19th century

Source: Adapted from a document produced by Santa Clara County (CA) Office of Education. The format for the lesson plan comes from Northview Public Schools (Grand Rapids, MI) and is outlined in *Better Learning Through Structured Teaching* (pp. 116–119), by D. Fisher and N. Frey, 2008, Alexandria, VA: ASCD.

- Using "I" statements, the teacher models his or her thinking aloud while performing a task.
- Teacher modeling examples are planned in advance.
- Modeling includes errors in order to model problem-solving strategies.
- Students witness what occurs when a problem-solving strategy does not work, including persistence and speculation about why it did not work.
- Students participate in the modeling, especially through student-to-student interactions.

Productive Group Work

- The task requires students to consolidate and extend their learning and not simply to copy what was modeled by the teacher.
- The task is designed so that there is the opportunity for productive failure, allowing students to wrestle with the content and requiring them to listen and negotiate with one another.
- The task is not easily subdivided among group members and then reassembled to complete the final task.
- Students interact with argumentation, not arguing.
- Students maintain joint attention to the materials that make up the task.

Guided Instruction

- The teacher is present and participatory.
- The lesson is directly related to the established purpose and the modeling phase of instruction.
- The teacher uses prompts, cues, and questions as scaffolds to help students find solutions.
- Prompts begin broadly ("Look on page 7…") and become more specific as needed ("In this paragraph on page 7, you'll be able to find the answer you're looking for").
- In small-group guided instruction, content, process, and/or product are differentiated to meet the learning goals of students.

Independent Learning

- The task is designed so that students draw extensively from previously learned material or skills.

- The task is controlled so that the new concepts students must apply are firmly established.

The Takeaway

After reading this chapter on quality core instruction, consider these key points:

- Quality core instruction is the foundation of RTI^2.
- A gradual release of responsibility model provides the room necessary for responsive teaching.
- This model of instruction requires establishing a purpose, teacher modeling, guided instruction, productive group work, and independent learning.
- High-quality core instruction averts unnecessary intervention supports.

4

Supplemental Interventions:
A Second-Level Defense

The school district that Nancy worked for in the 1990s adopted a new model to support impoverished schools using extra fiscal and human resources. The motto for this initiative was "unequal resources for unequal needs." At the time, one of Nancy's primary students seemed to consume an unequal amount of teacher time and attention due to some challenging behavior. Her other young charges sometimes complained (sweetly) that it "wasn't fair" that one of their classmates seemed to enjoy more of her time than others. Nancy briefly considered making a conceptual connection to the superintendent's initiative, but then remembered that these were children who still needed help zipping up their jackets. Instead, she talked to them about ear infections, something most 6-year-olds can relate to.

Most of the children had had a prescription for an antibiotic to treat an ear infection at some time in their lives, and they all agreed that it would be foolish to expect that they would have to share their prescription with everyone in the class. "But wouldn't that be fair?" asked Nancy. "Not everyone needs it!" they insisted. "Only the one who's got an ear infection." Nancy let their words hang in the air for a moment. "So what you're saying is that fair doesn't mean everyone gets the same. Fair means that everyone gets what they need." They nodded their heads in agreement. "So when someone in our class needs more of something, we should make sure that person gets it, right? Kind of like when I spend more time with one of you than the others. Because that's the right kind of fair."

Supplemental instruction is much like the medication that doctors order. The prescription comes only after a careful analysis of the symptoms and the patient's medical history. A treatment is prescribed, and the patient's progress is monitored. The dosage and duration of the treatment are determined in advance, but that doesn't preclude the doctor from running further tests if the medication does not seem to work.

RTI^2 follows a similar problem-solving path. First and foremost, it depends on the teacher's ability to observe outward signs of academic difficulty. Next, the teacher must be able to use assessments to capture the salient information needed to design effective interventions. The teacher's instructional design of the classroom should also support the implementation of supplemental instruction so that it aligns with core instruction. Finally, student progress should be monitored in order to gauge whether the intervention is effective.

The Role of Supplemental Instruction in RTI^2

Supplemental interventions, commonly referred to as Tier 2 interventions, are triggered when a student's progress slows to below expected levels. This gap is formally measured through benchmark assessments that are given at least three times per year. In truth, teachers are rarely surprised by the results of these assessments. Observant teachers are sensitive to signs of struggle and are aware that these signs may manifest themselves behaviorally before they are quantified with assessment instruments.

While there is debate surrounding the appropriate trigger point in determining whether a student should participate in supplemental intervention, most educators agree that an average score should serve as the benchmark. In the case of commercially prepared assessments, these benchmarks have been predetermined through a normative process. In other cases, such as with Abby in Chapter 2, the average of a random sample of five students in your class can provide an informal benchmark for comparing relative progress. You may recall that Abby's teacher compared Abby's progress to expected levels of learning acquisition by tracking weekly mastery of flashcards.

Another point of contention lies in determining what constitutes quality supplemental instruction. Instructional techniques vary widely, and, in many cases, supplemental instruction is teacher-designed. However, there is a growing field of commercially prepared products advertising their usefulness as a supplemental curriculum. While we do not have a problem with using commercially prepared (or, for that matter, teacher-designed) curricula, we do believe they should be carefully evaluated for quality indicators. Baker and colleagues' (2002) meta-analysis of effective mathematics interventions is instructive for any intervention. They advise that interventions should include

- A feedback mechanism for student and teacher to continuously foster learning gains.
- Peer interaction to further scaffold student understanding.
- Explicit instruction that emphasizes skill building.
- Contextualized instruction that emphasizes skills application.
- A process for informing parents of gains so that they can celebrate successes and offer praise and encouragement.

Moving from RTI to RTI^2 means looking closely at the quality of core instruction; supplemental *instruction* should occur, not just supplemental *intervention*. This requires an intentional blurring of what constitutes supplemental support available to students. We know that some students are prone to episodic difficulties—they occasionally fall behind due to illness or family situations, or they temporarily become overwhelmed by the content itself. Supplemental instruction and intervention means that there are safety nets in place for students who make progress, albeit fitfully. Accordingly, some Tier 2 supports discussed in this chapter are designed to meet the needs of those who are in need of episodic help.

As we noted in Chapter 2, supplemental instruction and interventions are different from quality core instruction because of their increased intensity, especially with regard to time, assessment, and expertise. It is essential to resist the temptation to swap them out for core instruction. Effective implementation of Tier 2 interventions affects the instructional design of the class. In addition, formal supplemental interventions must be of sufficient duration and frequency. More formalized supplemental interventions might include small-group lessons that occur at least three times per week, are sustained for at least 30 minutes per lesson, and endure for at least 20 weeks.

Increasing Intensity Through Group Size

A hallmark of supplemental instruction and intervention is that participating students are in small, similarly skilled groups (two to five members). When the teacher-student ratio is reduced to this size, teacher attention increases, which translates into increased opportunities to provide corrective feedback, scaffolded instruction, and collaborative peer learning experiences. In addition, the teacher can more easily check for understanding (Fisher & Frey, 2007a). The strategic use of cues, prompts, and questions inherent to guided instruction during Tier 1 quality core instruction is even more important in this setting.

Increasing Intensity Through Time

Figuring out where and when Tier 2 instruction and intervention will occur is a very real logistical concern for classroom teachers trying to structure their schedules so that students in need have access to help. If not artfully planned, Tier 2 interventions cease to be supplementary and become replacements for core instruction. Scheduling implications at the grade and school levels can either help or hinder delivery of Tier 2 instruction and intervention. Convenient times to implement Tier 2 supplemental instruction and intervention are

• During small-group, teacher-directed instruction when all students are engaged in collaborative and independent activities.
• During "zero period," a tutorial period scheduled before school.
• During lunchtime, like the Lunch Bunch that Adam belonged to in Chapter 1.
• During academic recovery sessions throughout the school day.
• During extended school times, including after-school tutorials, inter-session, and summer school.

Each of these options will be discussed in detail later in this chapter.

Increasing Intensity Through Assessment

The supplemental instruction and interventions needed in Tier 2 require assessment beyond the thrice-yearly benchmarks of Tier 1. Numerous reading assessments have already been mentioned; they include informal reading inventories that identify text at the student's instructional level and cloze procedure assessments that gauge semantic and syntactic knowledge. The cloze procedure is a passage completion task where every fifth word is deleted (Taylor, 1953). Some states, such as Texas, have specified assessment instruments for formal Tier 2 reading interventions. In a larger number of states, various curriculum-based measurements (CBMs) serve as the major method for monitoring progress and determining program design. Examples of CBMs include oral reading fluency rates, alphabetic knowledge, and phonemic awareness measures. In mathematics, CBMs include measures of number sense, computational fluency, and application tasks. In Tier 2 interventions, these measures are collected several times each month in order to keep a close eye on the learner's progress.

Increasing Intensity Through Expertise

The traditional model of remediation was that a child who was behind his or her peers would be separated from the rest of the class to work on reading or mathematics, usually with a paraprofessional or volunteer. Little attention was paid to other instruction that the student might be missing or whether the separation fostered social marginalization in the classroom. Another major problem with this model was that the person with the least amount of expertise often taught the students who needed the most help. This appraisal should not be interpreted as a criticism of paraprofessionals; in fact, we both began our educational careers as para-professionals. However, in too many cases, the paraprofessional's time was not used wisely. The best uses of paraprofessionals provide the teacher with more time to work with higher-needs students and support students achieving at or above grade level (Cobb, 2007). Put simply, the students who need the most help need more time with the person who has the most expertise—the classroom teacher.

The classroom teacher's expertise in meeting the needs of students in Tier 2 instruction and intervention can also be enhanced by consulta-tive relationships with other content experts. These experts include math coaches, reading specialists, Reading Recovery teachers, speech-language pathologists, and special educators on staff. Each has experience with harder-to-teach students and can offer advice on assessment, instructional routines, and motivational tools. At one school we work with, consultative visits are scheduled with RTI^2 team members who serve as in-class advi-sors. At the invitation of the classroom teacher, they observe and coach while the teacher meets with the student. These conversations are short but powerful, because the focus is on the instruction, not on other issues such as family support or previous educational experiences (topics that are better suited for RTI^2 committee meetings held after school).

Making Supplemental Instruction and Intervention Happen

Although there is widespread agreement that the promise of supplemental instruction and intervention will provide early supports for students who are falling behind and possibly prevent unnecessary special education referrals and placement, there are still logistical concerns. The questions of where and when to provide these supports are more easily addressed in elementary school than at the secondary level, but concerns remain across grades K–12 about how to make these supports truly supplementary without undercutting students' access to quality core instruction. The answer to the question of location seems to be to keep students in need of intervention physically in the classroom. Even the most conscientious teacher must admit that "out of sight is out of mind." As for when intervention should occur, especially in middle and high school, one solution is to lengthen the school day in order to provide the necessary and appropriate supports.

Small-Group Environments

As we discussed earlier in this chapter, small-group instruction with two to five students is effective because it decreases the teacher-student ratio while increasing interactions. This structure is beneficial for all students, not just those designated for further intervention supports (Foorman & Torgesen, 2001). Small-group math and science instruction at the high school level is particularly effective (Rice, 1999).

We have found that an easy way to implement small-group instruction and intervention is by using a Center Activity Rotation System, developed by our colleagues Diane Lapp, Jim Flood, and Kelly Goss (2000). Although originally conceived as a model for elementary classrooms, the concept also works well at the secondary level. Students are heterogeneously grouped for collaborative and independent activities that are typically completed without the teacher's assistance. While others are working, a teacher-directed group of students meets for guided instruction. These students are selected for guided instruction based on assessment data. Once they have finished, they return to their previous heterogeneous groups, and the teacher calls the next group of needs-alike students. On days when supplemental intervention occurs, the teacher meets with the Tier 2 group for an additional rotation. Because small-group instruction is a common feature of this classroom, the schedule is not disruptive for other students (see Figure 4.1). This approach is superior to the traditional method of keeping homogenous groups intact for collaborative and independent learning, because it does not unnecessarily impoverish less-skilled groups who may have fewer resources available to complete tasks.

Mr. Goldman uses a similar system in his 10th grade English class. A part of each day's class is dedicated to meeting with small groups whose members are reading different texts. He organizes his curriculum using essential questions, for example, "How do the tough get going?" Mr. Goldman explains, "We always have a focus text for the whole class. I'm leading the entire class in *The Grapes of Wrath* right now. I have my students in book clubs independently reading related literature that is closer to their reading levels." Mr. Goldman's more advanced readers are discussing Chinua Achebe's *Things Fall Apart*. Another group of four students is reading well below grade level, and their text is Francisco Jimenez's *The Circuit*. The books are united in theme, as each profiles characters who struggle with adversity in a changing culture. Mr. Goldman meets with the book clubs to discuss their reading but meets more frequently with the group reading *The Circuit* so that he can offer further instruction and intervention. Because this group struggles with reading comprehension, Mr. Goldman focuses his intervention time on that aspect. "We use the text for the intervention work because it doesn't make sense to introduce unrelated stuff," he says. The supplemental intervention lessons include oral fluency practice and applying problem-solving strategies to determine meaning when it is lost. "We've been joking that this is how the tough get going," he says. "The tough are resourceful!"

Students in Ms. DeBarge's kindergarten class have been learning about numerals and their values. It's early in the year, but most students have a steady grasp of the numbers up to 20. However, several students already show signs of falling behind. "I noticed it even before the first math benchmark assessment," she says. "I had a few who seemed unsure. They guessed a lot and weren't consistently naming numbers and values." She collected some informal math data and compared the results to the class average, which confirmed her suspicions. Because Ms. DeBarge uses small-group math instruction in her classroom, she is able to differentiate her teaching to meet her students' needs. She meets more frequently with the three students who are unsure about number values. "We play lots of games together, including flashcard games and ones that require manipulatives," she explains. "Ms. Tsai [a special educator] showed me last year how she uses a math balance to teach number value, so I'm doing

Figure 4.1
Center Activity Rotation System

8:30–8:45 a.m.: Teacher-directed core instruction for Group B
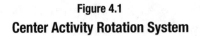

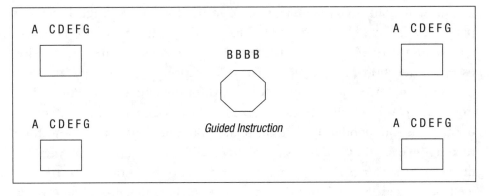

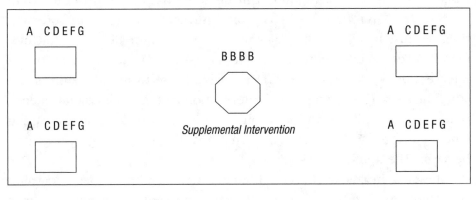

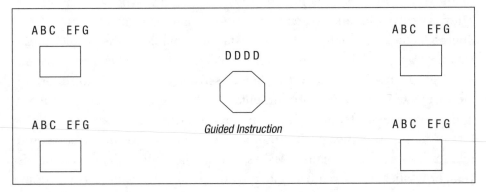

that, too." Ms. DeBarge actively collects data to monitor students' progress and give them feedback. "We make a little chart together every week so they can take it home to their families," she says. "I really appreciate the encouragement their parents offer the kids."

Academic Recovery

As part of a comprehensive RTI^2 system, specific students will need academic recovery to be successful. While some supplemental interventions are used for longer periods with individual students, academic recovery is for students who are at risk for not learning content as well as for students who periodically fall behind. One of the positive outcomes for schools that use academic recovery is that summative test scores are not affected when students experience episodic learning difficulties because the system immediately responds to ensure that students don't fall further behind and thus require additional supplemental, and sometimes intensive, interventions.

In many schools, there is a teacher responsible for academic recovery. Based on the size of the school, this can be a full-time release position funded via Title I or other compensatory education program. Schools that can afford a full-time staff member for academic recovery typically assign additional duties such as coordinating 504 plans, supervising tutorial services, or chairing the RTI^2 committee. In other words, the staff member focuses full-time on the design and delivery of supplemental interventions.

Successful academic recovery efforts serve as early warning systems. Accordingly, the educators responsible for academic recovery need access to assessment information and grades. As part of the job, the academic recovery staff member should systematically review report cards and grade books to determine if any students are at risk for failure.

Mr. Rankin serves as an academic recovery teacher at a high school and spends his time monitoring grade books electronically to identify students who suddenly, and sometimes unexpectedly, stop performing. For example, while reviewing biology grades, Mr. Rankin notices that Amanda did not complete her lab report and failed an exam in the same week. Amanda's previous performance was good, and she had a solid *B* in the class. Although her overall grade only dropped to a *B–*, and thus did not serve to alert her biology teacher, Mr. Rankin is concerned because he had provided support to Amanda the previous year. He makes a point to catch up with Amanda and find out what happened. Later that day, Mr.

Rankin learns that Amanda's father has been referred to an oncologist because his primary doctor suspected bone cancer. In addition to being scared, Amanda has added responsibilities at home, including babysitting her younger brother. Amanda and Mr. Rankin quickly complete a Grade Improvement Plan (see Figure 4.2) and agree to work together to keep Amanda's schoolwork at expected levels.

Not wanting Amanda to fall behind, Mr. Rankin offers to meet with her and a few other students who didn't do well on the test and to review the content with them. The biology teacher encourages students to review their tests and provides them with an opportunity to improve their grades by analyzing their incorrect responses, explaining why they got the answer wrong, and explaining why another answer is correct. Understanding her situation at home, Mr. Rankin reminds Amanda that her brother can stay for the after-school program at his elementary school or come to the high school with Amanda and attend the childcare center, go to the weight room, attend tutoring, or read quietly in their biology classroom.

Ms. Cooper has a similar academic recovery job at an elementary school. Like Mr. Rankin, Ms. Cooper spends her time focused on students who require supplemental intervention. As part of her role, she meets with every teacher during progress report time (not less often than every five weeks). During these conversations, Ms. Cooper and the classroom teacher identify students who might need "just in time" supplemental intervention. Of course, classroom teachers can initiate this type of support at any time; the meetings just formalize the process.

During one of these conversations, Ms. Cooper and a 5th grade teacher, Mr. Chapman, note Tyler's declining performance in mathematics. Mr. Chapman remarks, "He was doing well, but when we moved into graphing ordered pairs in the four quadrants of the coordinate plane, he started having trouble. He doesn't do the homework, which are familiar review problems. He does come to tutorial pretty regularly, and I've had him in small-group instruction several times this week. I think he needs a bit more to really understand this stuff."

The school has a well-developed homework system that provides a spiral review of content (Fisher & Frey, 2008). It does not focus on current course content, but it rather serves to reinforce content that students have learned in class. In 5th grade mathematics, students complete tasks using productive work groups and guided instruction before trying them individually at home. In Mr. Chapman's class, homework is based on content to which they have been exposed for at least three to five days. This

Figure 4.2
Grade Improvement Plan

Student Name: _____

Date of Conference: _____

Focus Area(s): _____

What am I having the most difficulty with in this class?

What do I need to do to raise my grade?	Who can help me?	Date

What is the first step in achieving my goal of academic recovery?

_____	_____	_____
Student Signature	Parent/Guardian Signature	Date
_____	_____	_____
Teacher Signature	Teacher Signature	Teacher Signature

approach provides students with increased competence and confidence as they complete familiar tasks at home. In addition, some of the homework serves to review content from previous weeks and months, allowing Mr. Chapman to continually assess student understanding.

However, in Tyler's current situation, both teachers understand that without additional supplemental intervention Tyler will not be successful and will be at risk for falling further behind. Ms. Cooper develops an Academic Intervention Plan (see Figure 4.3) and meets with Tyler. Given his previous success, and his participation in other supplemental interventions, the plan serves to

• Formalize the supplemental intervention system that is already in place.

• Communicate current concerns, actions that are taking place, and the importance of homework with Tyler's family.

• Allocate additional small-group instruction time for Tyler, to be delivered by either Mr. Chapman or Ms. Cooper.

Tutorials

In addition to—or as part of—academic recovery, some percentage of students may require access to tutorials. Tutorials can occur before school, during lunch, or after school. Tutorials can even take place during extended school year periods, such as intersession for year-round schools and summer school (i.e., instructional time for some students while others are "off track"). Many schools have access to funds such as Title I, targeted funding, donations, parent contributions, and foundation grants to operate tutorials. In general, tutorials involve small-group instruction and additional time on task. They differ from more intensive interventions in that they are not individualized and are rarely done in a one-to-one setting.

Regardless of the time of day they are delivered, highly effective tutorials incorporate certain characteristics (Desimone, 2002; Kane, 2004; Muñoz, Potter, & Ross, 2008), including

• Instruction from a credentialed teacher.

• Clear links to the core program, especially in terms of content standards.

• Content based on formative assessment information that demonstrates specific needs.

• A feedback system for families.

• Progress monitoring.

In many districts, tutorials are part of a larger learning contract. The learning contract (see Figure 4.4) serves as a communication tool and a way to formalize the engagement and participation expectations of each educational team member, including the student, his or her family or guardian, and the teachers.

Ms. Penrod meets with several of her 3rd grade students in the mornings before school. On any given day, there are about 12 students in the room. Ms. Penrod provides guided instruction for two to five students at a time. Much like the small-group instruction provided during the school day, students are grouped based on identified needs, and each session lasts for 15 to 20 minutes. The other students in the room work on computer programs that provide skills practice and reinforcement, read independently, or do homework. As each group finishes, Ms. Penrod calls a new group of students and focuses on their needs. This tutorial, for which Ms. Penrod receives compensation from the supplemental educational services provider in her district, has essentially provided students with additional time on task in a lesson that is tailored to specific instructional needs.

Supplemental interventions can also be provided at lunch, especially if the lunch period is lengthened a bit. Of course, students need time to eat and interact with peers, so most schools schedule students for this type of tutorial only once or twice per week. At one high school with a sophisticated RTI^2 initiative, teachers meet with students in need on a weekly basis. Mr. Mullins meets with students from his 9th grade English classes on Tuesdays, Ms. Poole meets with students from her world history class on Wednesdays, and Ms. Hobbs meets with students from her algebra class on Thursdays. When a student is recommended for more than two lunch tutorials, the teachers let the student pick which one(s) to attend, indicating the choice on his or her learning contract.

As we have noted, the focus of these tutorials must be clear so that learning can be aligned with curricular goals. It's not enough for Mr. Mullins to be available during lunch for students in need. Rather, he focuses his lunchtime tutorials on specific content standards and invites students to attend based on their performance with regard to those standards. For example, while teaching persuasive writing, Mr. Mullins identifies 29 students who are experiencing difficulty. Of those, 12 are already receiving supplemental and intensive interventions. Mr. Mullins invites the remaining 17 to lunch tutorial with him on Tuesdays. The focus of his tutorials is rapid review of the content, a concept that dates back to Frances Parker,

Figure 4.3
Academic Intervention Plan

Student Name: _____

Date of Conference: _____

Area(s) of Need: _____

```
┌─────────────────────────────────────────────────────────────┐
│ Concerns:                                                    │
│                                                              │
│                                                              │
│                                                              │
│                                                              │
│                                                              │
│                                                              │
│                                                              │
│                                                              │
│                                                              │
└─────────────────────────────────────────────────────────────┘
```

The student will
- ☐ Enter assignments into the agenda each class meeting.
- ☐ Find a homework partner and exchange numbers for information or clarification.
- ☐ Have a separate folder for homework and other assignments.
- ☐ Have a daily progress report signed.
- ☐ Have a weekly progress report signed.
- ☐ Print Power School grades weekly, and return them to the teacher with a parent's/guardian's signature.
- ☐ See an administrator _____. (how often)
- ☐ Meet with the teacher during lunch every **M Tu W Th F** at _____. (circle all that apply)

The parent/guardian will
- ☐ Provide a consistent and quiet place to do homework.
- ☐ Provide encouragement, motivation, and prompting.
- ☐ Provide reasonable time expectations.

The teacher/school will
- ☐ Post homework assignments on the school Web site and in class.
- ☐ Return corrected work to the student mailbox in a timely fashion.
- ☐ Provide missing homework.
- ☐ Initiate another student conference if progress is not seen.
- ☐ Initiate a family conference if progress is not seen.

_____	_____	_____
Student Signature	Parent/Guardian Signature	Date
_____	_____	_____
Teacher Signature	Teacher Signature	Teacher Signature

My Plan for Academic Recovery

What assignments are missing?	Targeted completion date

What help do I need to be successful?	Who can help me?	Date

How will I know if I am successful?

What is the first step in achieving my goal of academic recovery?

Figure 4.4

Learning Contract

Student Name: _____ ID No. _____

School: _____ Grade: _____

Teacher: _____ Year: _____

ASSESSMENT RESULTS

Literacy				Mathematics			
Assessments	Score	Level	Date	Assessments	Score	Level	Date
Stanford Diagnostic Reading Test (SDRT)				District mathematics test			
Analytical Reading Inventory (ARI)				Standards-Aligned Mathematics (SAM)			
CA Standards Test (CST)				CA Standards Test (CST)			
CA English Language Development Test (CELDT)				Teacher judgment (specify):			
Teacher judgment (specify):							

ACADEMIC INTERVENTIONS AND SUPPORTS

Literacy	Comments
☐ Daily guided instruction ☐ Extended-day reading program ☐ Extended-day science explorations through literacy ☐ Extended-day art explorations through literacy ☐ Summer school ☐ Intersession ☐ Saturday school ☐ Other: ☐ Student has active IEP or 504 plan for literacy ☐ Interventions/supports include a focus on ELD (ELLs only)	
Mathematics	**Comments**
☐ Daily guided instruction ☐ Extended-day mathematics program ☐ Summer school ☐ Intersession ☐ Saturday school ☐ Other: ☐ Student has an active IEP or 504 plan for mathematics ☐ Interventions/supports include SDAIE methodology (ELLs only)	

Figure 4.4—(*continued*)
Learning Contract

How teacher(s)/counselor will communicate student progress to parent/guardian:

☐ Progress reports   ☐ Telephone calls   ☐ Notes   ☐ Follow-up conferences   ☐ E-mail
☐ Other:

Student: Your signature below indicates that you understand your responsibilities and commit to actively participating in the support programs that the teacher recommends to help you become successful and prepared for the next grade.

Parent/guardian: Your signature below indicates that you understand your responsibilities and commit to the interventions and supports described for your student's academic improvement.

Teacher(s): Your signature below indicates that you understand your responsibilities and will provide instruction based on student needs, suggest ways the parent/guardian can support learning at home, and report the student's progress to the parent/guardian on an ongoing basis.

Student's Signature	Parent's/Guardian's Signature	Teacher's Signature

Date _____

☐ After repeated attempts, the school was unable to communicate directly with the parent/guardian.

who noted of an effective teacher: "Each day, before taking up the new lesson, she makes a rapid review of all the lessons they have already read from the chart; in this way giving to them gradually the ability to read the print without the immediate aid of a script" (1886, p. 120).

These rapid review lessons help students who are at risk of falling behind. Of course, these lunch tutorials do not solely constitute a comprehensive supplemental intervention effort, but they are part of an overall effort to address students' needs as they arise. Of the 17 students who participate in the lunch tutorials, 16 of them soon demonstrate mastery of the content. One student, Kyanna, does not, so it is determined that she needs additional supplemental interventions.

After-School Tutorial and Enrichment Programs

Given the lack of progress Mr. Mullins sees in Kyanna, in terms of both the core instruction and the lunch tutorial, he recommends that she participate in an additional after-school tutorial. The after-school program, funded with federal 21st Century Learning Community money, provides extended-day programs and services in three areas: (1) standards-based academic support, (2) enrichment activities that allow students to explore connections between academics and the world, and (3) site-based ongoing and accessible family literacy services that promote community involvement (U.S. Department of Education, 2009). Students who attend the after-school program enjoy a wide range of opportunities that focus on academic areas such as reading, literacy, mathematics, and science. These activities include but are not limited to

- Extended school library hours (until 8:00 p.m.) four days per week.
- Tutoring in content-area classes from 2:45–4:45 p.m., four days per week.
- Daily small-group reading tutoring.
- Extended computer lab hours (until 6:00 p.m.) four days per week.
- Academic support classes for English language learners three days per week.
- Daily peer tutoring and teacher-facilitated mentoring activities five days per week.
- A weekly entrepreneurial business management class.
- A "Young Articulators" public speaking and writing class two days per week.
- A homework assistance center staffed by teachers until 6:00 p.m. daily.
- A test review class focused on the high school exit exam.
- Weekly financial literacy classes.

In addition, students can participate in a wide range of enrichment and support activities that focus on nutrition and health, art, music, drama, technology, and recreation, including

- African drumming classes.
- Choir and musical instrument practice.
- Nutrition and cooking classes.
- Child development classes.
- Drama classes (including writing and play production).
- Hip-hop dance and DJ operations classes.

- Sports clinics (including rock wall climbing and in-line skating).
- Self-defense classes.
- Driver's education.
- Artist's workshop.
- Online teen publications.
- Fitness center access until 8:00 p.m.

The combination of after-school supplemental intervention efforts with student-oriented enrichment activities increases the attention the after-school program receives from all students, not just those who need academic assistance.

Kyanna attends the after-school program four days per week. She participates in daily tutoring and small-group reading. Following her academic time in the program, Kyanna often stays for hip-hop dance and cooking classes. The added time on task—in a program provided by teachers—results in Kyanna developing her persuasive writing skills to a level on par with the rest of her class.

Extended-Year Programs

Tutorials can also be delivered through intersession and summer school programs. As with other types of tutorials, it's essential that intersession and summer school are directly linked with the core curriculum and that they continue the instruction specific students need to master content standards. Unfortunately, this isn't always the case. In some districts, intersession and summer school programs operate as stand-alone activities, focusing on a curriculum that is completely separate from the regular school experience. The outcomes for these types of programs are predictable: students fall further behind in their core classes and, in some cases, have to make up work from the summer program.

Paul, a "strategic" student, knows that he can fail a couple classes each year and take them in summer school. He finds it preferable to attend and pass the five-week version of a class that he doesn't like very much than to make the effort during the school year. When asked about his experience, Paul says, "I just kinda give up when it gets hard. I can take the easy version later and be fine." Indeed, this tactic worked for him throughout middle school.

However, his high school does not offer a traditional summer school option. Instead, as part of their RTI[2] efforts, the teachers essentially extend the school year rather than offer entirely new summer courses. Of course, they also use academic recovery and tutorials during the school year to prevent students from needing the extended school year program at all.

Paul is surprised when, just five weeks into the year, he meets with a teacher who develops a learning contract with him for his math class. In addition to small-group instruction during class, Paul attends tutorials after school several times each week. He makes progress over the course of the year and demonstrates his knowledge on every standard except solving quadratic equations by factoring. By the end of the year, Paul still has not demonstrated mastery of this one concept, and his grade is low as a result.

As part of his learning contract, Paul and his family agree to an extended school year if Paul does not master the course content with at least a *B*. Paul has no problem agreeing to this; he has attended summer school nearly every year of his academic life. This summer, however, is different. Given that he has only one area of need, Paul spends several hours each day during extended school year working on that content. He has access to small-group instruction, one-to-one intervention, progress monitoring, and feedback. After just four days, he passes a competency exam on which he demonstrates his knowledge of solving quadratic equations by factoring, and his grade is updated accordingly. At that point, Paul is invited to participate in a number of summer enrichment opportunities. He chooses Commonsense Self-Defense and Physics of Extreme Sports, classes funded by the 21st Century Learning Community grant at his school. At the end of the summer program, Paul comments, "I never knew summer could be like this. Those classes were sick [awesome]. Like, instead of suffering, I learned karate and skateboarding. Next year, no more makeup for me."

Accommodations: Learning from the Responses of Students with Disabilities

Although RTI[2] is not a special education initiative—it is used in part to prevent unnecessary referrals to special education—there are clear parallels to best practices for students with disabilities. Within every classroom are students with Individual Education Programs (IEPs) who participate in the general education curriculum. In some cases, this participation is made meaningful through the use of curricular and instructional accommodations. It is not lost on us, as educators, that these practices are consistent with the work of Carol Ann Tomlinson and others on differentiated instruction (e.g., Tomlinson & Strickland, 2005), and that these techniques can also be used as supplemental intervention for students without identified disabilities.

Although a useful IEP should articulate practices that have met with past success, we often encounter forms with an extensive menu of accommodations. These checklists seem to encourage a buffet line response—"I'll have a little of this, and oh, that looks good!"—rather than evidence-based decision making. A categorization system can make the bewildering lists of accommodations more meaningful and in turn make delivering the accommodations more authentic and effective. A well-structured RTI^2 system has the added benefit of offering an instructional design through which accommodations become classroom support for students with and without identified disabilities. These accommodations should flow from the overall design of the class and not merely be bolted on as an afterthought.

One of the best categorizations of curricular and instructional accommodations was described by Cole and colleagues (2000). Some categories will seem familiar in light of the content we have already covered, and that is how it should be.

Time Accommodations

The most frequently used testing accommodation listed on state policy documents is extended time (Bolt & Thurlow, 2004). Adjustments may be made to the time allotted for a task, assignment, or test. For example, in Mr. Jefferson's 7th grade social studies class, Vicente's IEP provides him with an extended deadline of an extra three days to complete his project on life in medieval Japan. Vicente's extended time accommodation comes with conditions: he must work on his project in class when others are doing so, and he has to set up a timeline for completion with his teacher. Time as an accommodation is used carefully at this school. "We don't give kids an unlimited calendar," Mr. Jefferson says. "After all, the school year does come to an end."

Size Accommodations

Along with time, size is a commonly used accommodation for students with disabilities. Often, time and size accommodations are paired in order to create tasks that are aligned with course content. For instance, 9th grade algebra teacher Ms. Taylor differentiates Jaylene's problem sets in class. "She's able to do the problems, but at a slower pace," Ms. Taylor explains. "I'll select particular problems for her to focus on. She's in a collaborative group of five students who work on the problems together. I usually have her work on three of the four assigned problems, which gives her extra time to review her work before we return to the whole class."

Input Accommodations

Students with mild disabilities in a general education classroom are responsible for learning the content of a course, but they may use alternative means for accessing the information. The relatively recent availability of affordable technology accommodations has given classroom teachers new ways to deliver information. For example, the earth science textbook for Mr. Kichener's course comes with a DVD that allows students to listen to the text read aloud. "They can even choose a male or female voice," he chuckles. "It's an accommodation I use for several students in my class, including a few who don't have IEPs." Mr. Kichener uses this input accommodation to support a few students who are reading below grade level, as well as two students who are identified as English language learners.

Of course, not all input accommodations rely on technology. "I first began posting key points on the board at the beginning of the lesson years ago, when it was required as an input accommodation for a girl I had in my class," says 5th grade teacher Ms. Horne. "I noticed that it worked well for other kids, too, and now it's just part of the routine."

Output Accommodations

In much the same way that input accommodations are designed to alter the ways in which information is received, output accommodations alter the way a student demonstrates his or her mastery of concepts or skills. As with all other accommodations, the student is held to the same standards-based content knowledge. However, the learner may demonstrate understanding in a teacher-led conversation or in an oral report to the class, instead of in a written essay. Alicia circles the answers to her weekly science quiz in her 3rd grade class rather than write the answer on the corresponding line across from the question. "Visually, it seems to keep her organized," says her teacher, Ms. Rowan. "The thing I care most about is whether she knows the content. Understanding that energy has multiple forms and can be changed is a 3rd grade science standard," she explains. "Being able to write the letters on the line isn't."

Level of Support Accommodations

Much of the learning that comes from a gradual release of responsibility model occurs through productive group work. The collaborative phase is built for fostering peer supports among students. Some teachers are concerned that reliance on peer supports is detrimental to the learning of the student who offers support, but keep in mind that Vygotsky's work on the Zone of Proximal Development (1978) involved the learning that occurs within a child who assists his or her peers. Take the case of Carla and Beatriz, two 2nd grade students in Ms. Collins's mathematics class. Beatriz often discusses the written and oral directions with Carla, who has an IEP and is an English language learner. She and Beatriz share a common first language, and hearing the directions repeated in Spanish is helpful for Carla. At the same time, Beatriz continues to build her academic language skills in both languages as she explains the directions to her friend.

These five categories of accommodations—time, size, input, output, and level of support—are commonly used in designing special education supports, but many can easily be extended to students without disabilities who are participating in Tier 2 or Tier 3 interventions. By offering simple accommodations that remove barriers to learning, students at risk for failure benefit from an additional safety net. None of these accommodations affects *what* students learn, only *how* they learn it. A list of accommodations appropriate for students without disabilities can be found in Figure 4.5.

The Takeaway

After you have read this chapter, consider the following key points:

• Providing every student with the same thing as every other student isn't fair; providing each student with what he or she needs is fair.

• Supplemental instruction must be aligned with high-quality core instruction.

• Supplemental instruction allows for increased intensity in terms of group size, time, assessments, and expertise.

• There are a number of ways to increase the time students spend in learning environments, including before-school, lunchtime, and after-school tutorials.

• Knowledge of accommodations for students with disabilities can be used to support the learning of students in need of supplemental intervention.

Figure 4.5

Accommodations for Students Without Disabilities

Type of Accommodation	Examples
Time	• Extend time by 50 percent on assignments. • Offer an untimed test. • Restructure tasks so that students who need support finish at the same time as students who are assigned the original task. • Assign a take-home test.
Size	• Reduce the number of questions by selecting representative items. • Provide a "main idea" version of a longer piece of informational text.
Input	• Enlarge font or increase the amount of white space on the page. • Underline or highlight directions. • Provide notes, study guides, or copies of a presentation. • Color-code important words or phrases. • Provide advance notice of assignments. • Identify alternative readings on the same topic.
Output	• Allow voice-recorded responses. • Supply sentence frames so that students can insert appropriate words or phrases. • Allow students to circle the correct answer rather than write the corresponding letter. • Provide sample sentences for use as a model. • Use manipulatives to complete math assignments. • Assign an open-book test.
Level of Support	• Provide a peer tutor or cross-age tutor. • Supply paraprofessional support and redirection. • Use paired or partner reading. • Chunk assignments into smaller tasks to complete. • Use an agenda or assignment journal to keep track of due dates. • Provide family members with a copy of assignments in advance.

5

Intensive Interventions for High-Risk Learners:

Mobilizing Experts and Resources

Third grade student Natalie arrives at the classroom door to meet with intervention specialist Ms. Espinoza. Natalie has her social studies textbook under one arm, and she begins talking excitedly. "We're learning about the American Indian tribes that lived here!" Ms. Espinoza knows this and has stayed in close communication with Natalie's teacher in order to align her intervention lessons with classroom learning. "I know!" Ms. Espinoza replies. "That's why I chose this reading on the Wampanoag. They settled this area long ago and are an important part of our community today." Natalie is participating in a Tier 3 intervention because her reading comprehension is significantly behind other students her age.

Ms. Espinoza begins by showing Natalie several images from the local historical society that depict the daily life of the Wampanoag at the time of English settlement. She then models her thinking while she reads an introductory paragraph aloud from the social studies book. She asks Natalie to think aloud as they continue to read together about life in a Wampanoag village. Natalie and Ms. Espinoza revisit the previous chapter of the social studies book to recall a similar passage on daily life in nearby Plymouth Plantation. Using a Venn diagram, Natalie locates details that compare and contrast the two passages. Over the next 30 minutes, Natalie and Ms. Espinoza discuss the content and the strategies to employ when reading becomes difficult. Ms. Espinoza informs Natalie, "You can use this in your social studies class this week, and you'll know a lot about the Wampanoag and the English. Just use your graphic organizer." Ms. Espinoza knows that it's important for Natalie to get instruction and intervention. The goal is for her to apply reading techniques in the classroom, and a good way to achieve this is to make sure the Tier 3 and core lessons relate to each other.

Why Intensive Intervention?

Tier 3 interventions are distinguished from Tier 2 by further intensification of time, expertise, and assessment. This level of intervention is notable for its increased duration (more than 20 weeks), frequency (often five times per week), and decreased group size (individual). While more complex to offer, one-to-one instruction has proven its merit in the research. For instance, Vellutino and Scanlon (2001) compared the progress of more than 100 1st grade students who had participated in either small-group or one-to-one instruction. Their findings indicated that children in the one-to-one grouping arrangement achieved, on average, at the 45th percentile on measures of reading, compared to the 19th percentile for those in the small-group arrangement. Of course, individual instruction has long been a hallmark of related support services and is used extensively in reading clinics, by speech-language pathologists, by occupational therapists, and in academic tutoring environments.

Conditions Necessary for Effective Intensive Intervention Efforts

A review of intervention efforts by Fisher and Ivey (2006) suggests that at least five factors must be considered for interventions to matter: (1) the teacher should play a critical role in assessment and instruction, (2) the intervention should reflect a comprehensive approach to reading and writing, (3) the intervention should be engaging, (4) interventions should be driven by useful and relevant assessments, and (5) interventions should include significant opportunities for authentic reading and writing. Figure 5.1 contains a rubric that can be used to evaluate the implementation of each of these factors. It must be noted, however, that these factors are based on specific conditions that must already be in place for intervention efforts to be effective.

Figure 5.1

Analysis of Interventions

	5	4	3	2	1
Do the intervention initiatives cause students to read more and to read better?					
Teachers are actively involved in providing intervention and support.	There is significant teacher involvement in the design and delivery of the intervention.		There is some teacher oversight, but the majority of the program is delivered by volunteers or paraprofessionals.		There is limited or no teacher involvement; intervention is delivered in the absence of a teacher (e.g., computer-only programs or take-home workbooks).
Intervention reflects a comprehensive approach to reading and writing.	Intervention is comprehensive and integrated such that students experience reading and writing as a cohesive whole.		Intervention includes important components of the reading process but addresses them separately (e.g., 15 minutes of word study followed by an unrelated comprehension activity); either reading or writing is addressed, but not both.		Intervention focuses on an isolated skill (e.g., topic sentence) or a single aspect of literacy development (e.g., phonics, phonemic awareness, fluency, vocabulary, comprehension).
Intervention reading and writing is engaging.	Authentic children's and adolescent literature (fiction and nonfiction) is at the core of the intervention.		Program uses isolated paragraphs on selected topics.		Program uses artificial text, no connected text, or skills work.
Intervention instruction is driven by useful and relevant assessments.	Teacher-administered assessments are ongoing and used to tailor individual instruction; writing samples and text-based discussions are one type of assessment used.		Uniform assessments are used for placement, program entry, and program exit.		All students start at the same point and move through the intervention components in the same way regardless of their individual performance.
Intervention includes significant opportunities for authentic reading and writing.	The majority of intervention time is devoted to authentic reading and writing.		Periodic opportunities are provided for students to read or write.		No connected reading and writing is provided or required (e.g., sole focus on word-level activities or skills worksheets).

Source: From *Creating Literacy-Rich Schools for Adolescents*, by G. Ivey and D. Fisher, 2006, Alexandria, VA: ASCD. Adapted with permission.

Condition 1: High-Quality Core Program

As we have noted repeatedly, interventions cannot compensate for ineffective core programs. Even a 60-minute individualized intervention of very high quality will yield only minor results if the remaining five hours (or more) of the school day are wasted because the tasks are too difficult or not differentiated for a student who performs significantly below grade level. The result is that the student is "learning" for only about an hour a day, while other members of the class are learning for six hours per day. As Allington puts it, "Struggling readers struggle more because they get far less appropriate instruction every day than the achieving students do" (2009, p. 2).

Condition 2: Access to Expert Teachers

To be effective, intensive intervention efforts should be developed and delivered by experts. It's important to remember that students who receive Tier 3 intensive intervention need access to teachers with *more* expertise, not less. Unfortunately, in far too many situations, intensive interventions are provided by computers, volunteers, or paraprofessionals. Obviously, computers can't interact with learners in the same way that a professional can, and expert interaction is exactly what students who are seriously behind really need. As Allington reminds us, "A large body of research indicates that paraprofessionals do little that actually improves a student's reading achievement in classrooms of either remedial or special education programs" (2009, p. 7). To ensure that intensive interventions are effective, the first thing that schools and districts need to figure out is how they can utilize experts in their intensive intervention efforts.

Condition 3: Individual Instruction

At this tier, students need—*deserve*—individualized one-to-one instruction. While most students in a school make progress in the core program, and some students need supplemental intervention, there are students for whom individual instruction is necessary. The practice of a knowledgeable adult offering instruction to an individual student has been a valued approach in education, although many teachers report that they rarely have time to provide such an experience (Moody, Vaughn, & Schumm, 1997). A meta-analysis of 31 studies of one-to-one reading tutoring programs found that "well-designed, reliably implemented, one-to-one interventions can make significant contributions to improved reading outcomes for many students whose poor reading skills place them at risk for academic failure" (Elbaum, Vaughn, Hughes, & Moody, 2000, p. 617). This finding is consistent with a similar study of five one-to-one reading intervention programs conducted earlier (Wasik & Slavin, 1993) and recommendations for success in mathematics (Karp & Howell, 2004).

Components of an Effective Intensive Intervention Effort

With these conditions met, we can focus on the components of the intensive intervention itself. First, we assume that schools looking for intervention programs to supplement their efforts already provide students with significant opportunities for wide reading. By this, we mean that students have access to a substantial number of readable, interesting books that focus on the content they are studying. In other words, students are reading things they *can* read to build their vocabulary and background knowledge on a given subject. We also mean that students are provided the opportunity to "just read" books of their own choosing (Fisher, 2004; Worthy, Broaddus, & Ivey, 2001). The power of addressing such a fundamental condition for literacy development can be seen in the changes experienced by students and teachers at Western High School (Fisher, Frey, & Lapp, 2009). Responding to assessments that indicated nearly all students were reading one or more grade levels below their placement, Western High implemented several initiatives, including sustained silent reading, Cornell note taking, shared reading, and writing to learn. These initiatives, especially the wide reading, yielded notable increases in students' achievement and motivation to read.

Second, we assume that the entire school is focused on literacy achievement and that teachers use content literacy approaches to ensure that their students are engaged in a meaningful curriculum. By this, we mean that during history, science, math, English, art, music, and so on, teachers ensure that students are developing strategic reading skills as they read for information (Ivey, 2004). Tubman High School in San Diego, California, experienced a 12 percent overall gain in statewide achievement tests over a two-year period as three trends took shape in classrooms across content areas (Fisher, 2001). First, staff development for all teachers focused on specific instructional routines (e.g., K-W-L, writing to learn, concept mapping, reciprocal teaching) that students experienced consistently among different content areas. Second, schools provided daily independent reading time and purchased large quantities of books specifically for this initiative. Third, teachers implemented block scheduling to better facilitate reading and writing opportunities and instruction across all content area classes.

Without these nonnegotiable features of the learning environment—access to high-quality, readable texts and instruction in cognitive strategies for reading and writing throughout the school day—it is doubtful that a specific, limited intervention will make much difference. If a school has already made these fundamental changes and there are still students who struggle to read, it is likely that an intervention program or initiative is necessary. Although any number of programs can be considered, we suggest that the people who have the power to purchase, implement, or develop a program consider the following factors.

The Teacher Should Play a Critical Role in Assessment and Instruction

A common ingredient in case studies of struggling readers who demonstrate considerable improvement is significant time spent with an expert teacher (e.g., McCormick, 1994; Morris, Ervin, & Conrad, 1996). In fact, it is difficult to find intervention success stories that do not feature teacher involvement in a major way. When we refer to teacher involvement, we suggest something that extends far beyond the general notion of individualization. Certainly, there are many programs that differentiate materials and assignments for students, but they do not necessarily personalize the *instruction*.

We know of plenty of commercially available programs that advertise individualized learning, but what does that mean? It might mean that students get texts at different levels, that they work alone at a computer at their own pace, or that they are grouped according to ability levels. What is different about the *teaching*, though, and how is it connected to individual students? It is highly unlikely that a computer, for example, could accurately evaluate a student's strengths and needs or tend to the complexity of individual students' motivations for reading and writing (Alvermann & Rush, 2004). Only expert teachers are in a place to make split-second decisions that facilitate student understanding of the text and knowledge about literacy processes (Johnston, 1987).

Consider Jessie, a 6th grade student who participates in a one-to-one tutoring session with Ms. Frausto, a reading specialist. Jessie's class is working on information reports, and her teacher wants to make sure that

Jessie has practice with relating information in sequence. Jessie reads at roughly a 3rd grade level and enjoys sequence stories, especially sequence stories that have crazy or silly endings such as *Ring! Yo?* and *The Napping House*. On this day, Ms. Frausto introduces Jessie to *The House That Jack Built*. After talking about the book cover and the illustrations to help her organize her thinking about the book, Jessie starts reading.

While reading, she comes to the word *malt*. She says the word correctly but looks confused and stops reading. Jessie has no apparent cognitive strategies for moving on. Ms. Frausto tells Jessie that sometimes when she's reading, she skips an unfamiliar word, reads the next several words, and then makes a guess about the word in question using the meaning of the sentence and any clues the author provides, such as illustrations. On the next page of the story, the word *malt* is used again, and there is an illustration of a rat eating something from a large bag. Jessie says, "I guess that stuff coming out of the bag is malt, right? I was thinking of Dairy Queen and the drink, so I was confused." Ms. Frausto clarifies the definition of malt as a grain.

Several pages later, Jessie comes to the word *worried* and pauses. This time she reads on but can't find any clues that help her. She slowly starts to pronounce the word—"Wooorrry"—and thinks she is correct. "Oh, it says 'that worry the cat.'" Ms. Frausto asks Jessie to look at the end of the word and reminds her that all of the other actions in the story were past tense. Jessie quickly self-corrects and says, "Oh, I mean, 'that worried the cat.'"

It isn't our goal to focus extensively or exclusively on a reading lesson in this section, but rather to point out that the teacher is critical to this exchange. Without the teacher present and participating, it is impossible to know where Jessie is getting stumped and what needs to be explained to her (Duffy, 2003). When we implement programs that fail to prominently feature teachers' expertise, we are likely leaving students' learning to chance.

Interventions Should Reflect a Comprehensive Instructional Approach

We often see an either/or theme among reactions to poor reading achievement. It is assumed, for example, that persistent reading problems are the result of deficiencies in either word-level skills or comprehension skills. Certainly, we know of students with obvious problems in word recognition and others who can read every word but not remember or understand what they read. If things were really as simple as this either/or approach implies, we would have solved the problem of persistent reading problems long ago, because a plethora of programs aimed at "fixing" specific reading difficulties has existed for decades. Such programs seem to be rising in popularity, despite a lack of solid evidence that they make much of a difference.

One belief underlying the skill-by-skill, piecemeal approach to learning to read is that once students learn all the necessary skills for reading and writing, they will magically put it all together. It is certainly possible to find research that indicates teaching a particular skill increases aptitude with that skill, but does that make the student a better or more motivated reader? All students need to see the big picture when it comes to reading and writing, and good interventions should begin with reading, writing, listening to, and thinking about meaningful texts. Instruction in the processes of reading and writing (e.g., word recognition, comprehension strategies, vocabulary, fluency) ought to help facilitate students' engagement with and understanding of real texts, rather than take center stage in the program.

Our colleague Diane Lapp makes the following analogy to a sailing manual, which reads, "Bend to boom and attach outhaul." You can take a phonics-only approach to the sentence and decode each word, but it will not result in understanding. If you likewise were to take a vocabulary-only approach, learning the multiple meanings of each word, the text still wouldn't make sense. Similarly, if you took a fluency-only approach and practiced the sentence faster and faster, you still wouldn't understand it. Understanding a sentence like this one requires background knowledge, decoding, vocabulary, fluency, and cognitive strategies. Students have to learn to mobilize each of these at the right time. To really focus on comprehension, the other processes need to be automatic, which only comes with considerable practice.

Brandon is a struggling 9th grade student who reads far below grade level. Reading specialists have indicated that he reads at a 1st grade level. The problem with this comparison is that he has a lot more experience than a 1st grade student and uses that knowledge, for better or worse, every time he reads. We are reminded of Luke (Ivey & Fisher, 2006), whose street knowledge outpaced his reading skill. Luke's teacher invited him to read a book "matched to his reading level," Joy Cowley's *Dan, the Flying Man*—a simple picture book that one would likely find in a kindergarten classroom. When he read the title, Luke looked up, obviously perplexed, and asked, "Do you think he's on drugs?" It did not even occur to Luke that his teacher would give him a book that made higher-order reasoning unnecessary. *Dan, the Flying Man* was no match for this teen's knowledge base and his ability—and desire—to think critically.

Brandon's poor reading levels interfere with achievement in all of his classes. Thankfully, he has access to books he can read in each class, which facilitates his understanding of the content. He also participates in a number of supplemental interventions, but he clearly needs individualized instruction. The assessment information points to the fact that Brandon is a curriculum casualty. He has been to a number of different schools and has not experienced success in any of them. He's been undertaught. A quick review of his record suggests that he's been in and out of different intervention programs, mostly ones that focused on only one aspect of literacy at a time. What Brandon hasn't been able to do is put it all together and really learn to read. He's a word-caller who reads somewhat slowly and doesn't understand what he reads.

Brandon's intervention teacher, Ms. Dixon, sees him daily for 30 minutes during English class and weekly for an hour after school. She starts her efforts with the Language Experience Approach, an instructional routine more than 40 years old (Ashton-Warner, 1959; Dixon & Nessel, 1983). Brandon is invited to share his thoughts on a given topic, and Ms. Dixon writes his thoughts on a small dry-erase board. Brandon copies the sentences into his notebook and continues expanding upon the ideas with his own writing. This is a good approach for Brandon, and he quickly gets to see the relationships between the various components of reading and writing. He also benefits from practice with the content standards of his classes and produces writing he can submit to his teachers.

During one of the sessions, Brandon and Ms. Dixon talk about his earth science class. Brandon clearly knows a lot about tectonic plates and likes to discuss earthquakes and volcanoes. As they speak about various earthquakes from California's history, Brandon explains that the lithosphere is the earth's crust and the top part of the mantle. Impressed with his understanding, Ms. Dixon asks Brandon to repeat himself so that they can write a sentence. Through some give-and-take, in which Ms. Dixon scaffolds his word choice and has him rehearse the sentence several times, Brandon produces and writes the following sentence:

> The lithosphere is the uppermost part of the mantle and represents the earth's surface.

Ms. Dixon writes this on her dry-erase board, and they spend a few minutes talking about the spelling of the word *mantle*, the meaning of *uppermost*, and the possessive apostrophe. She then invites Brandon to copy this sentence into his earth science notebook and write a few more sentences about the topic. As expected, his independent sentences aren't as sophisticated as the ones he shares with Ms. Dixon orally. This, however, is part of the apprenticeship—he will slowly incorporate sophisticated language into his writing. The gradual process will help him read more and read better. Brandon writes:

> The mantle be hard. It move in earthquakes and can brake.

Ms. Dixon knows that this type of intentional instruction is essential for Brandon to see the relationship between ideas and printed words. He also needs considerable practice with language, reading, and writing. Ms. Dixon knows that, as Brandon becomes increasingly skilled, she will begin sharing the pen with him so that he can write immediately following their conversations. Of course, she'll still focus on various aspects of language such as spelling, word meaning, fluency, and comprehension. This comprehensive approach is what has been missing from Brandon's educational life for many years.

Interventions Should Be Engaging

It is not difficult to find interventions that even struggling or resistant students will find interesting and engaging. After all, most programs are designed to offer instruction and materials that are below grade level and target the whole class; for students who consistently struggle with most reading and writing experiences, this is a welcome relief. In other words, some interventions get normally noncompliant students to suddenly be amenable to classroom activities. Observing this type of change, however, may falsely lead to the belief that the intervention is working and the students are learning.

In order to see measurable gains in achievement and motivation outside of the intervention, instruction and materials need to be engaging, as Guthrie cautions:

When children read merely to complete an assignment, with no sense of involvement or curiosity, they are being compliant. They conform to the demands of the situation irrespective of their personal goals. Compliant students are not likely to become lifelong learners. (1996, p. 433)

When we inundate older struggling readers with superficial and lifeless tasks that bear no resemblance to the reading and writing they encounter in the real world, we practically ensure their status as outsiders to the literate community. It is difficult to find studies of literacy these days that do not highlight the critical role of engagement and, particularly, the importance of using interesting reading materials (e.g., Ivey & Broaddus, 2001; Worthy, Moorman, & Turner, 1999).

Remember that most students who participate in intensive interventions have had negative, or at least unproductive, school experiences. Remember Adam, our "choose your adventure" subject from Chapter 1? In one option, Adam's experiences were counterproductive to his learning. Perhaps even more important, they were harmful to future intervention efforts. As students repeatedly experience failure and a lack of relevance, they become harder to engage in subsequent years.

Eleventh grade student Patrick is a prime example of this. It took his teaching team two full years to reengage him in learning. Ms. Allen, the teacher who directs intervention efforts at his school, says that it remains a daily struggle to ensure that Patrick learns. He had so many experiences with various efforts that eventually failed him that he inevitably gave up. A quick look at his middle school transcripts clearly demonstrates this—all *F*s, except P.E., in which he earned a *B*.

What did it ultimately take to help Patrick learn and subsequently pass all of his classes? In addition to a supportive group of professionals who genuinely cared about him and his success, Patrick needed to be actively engaged. He had to see the relevance in the tasks he was asked to do, and he needed interventions that made him feel successful and built his confidence. For Patrick, this came when teachers provided him with tasks he understood. Patrick said that he finally understood algebra and geometry, and then passed the high school exit exam, because of the projects he completed in class and as part of the intervention efforts. He described one of his proudest academic moments as follows:

We had to make this arch. I never worked so hard before, ever. I really wanted it to stay up, and I made it over and over so it could. When it fell down, we had to solve why. That took some equations and stuff. I did 'em with Ms. Allen, and we both learned why it fell and got back to work trying to make it stand up. I never worked so hard, especially on equations. Then I got them, and the equations worked, and I could do them in class.

Interventions Should Be Driven by Useful and Relevant Assessments

Countless research studies and individual student descriptions from recent years (e.g., Ivey, 1999; Riddle Buly & Valencia, 2002; Rubenstein-Avila, 2003/2004) present an instructional challenge that is difficult to ignore: struggling readers are extremely complex, and in order to meet their needs, we must take a closer and more sophisticated look at their literacy strengths, needs, and preferences. This means that, in addition to quality initial assessments (e.g., informal reading inventories, spelling inventories, writing samples, interviews, observations), ongoing assessments are necessary to determine if students understand the varied purposes for reading and writing, which skills they have already mastered, and where they could use further assistance.

To fully appreciate students' needs within an intervention, educators need to see them engage in literacy tasks in a variety of contexts (including diverse print and electronic reading materials) and for a variety of purposes (including reasons for reading and writing outside of school). It is doubtful that paying close and deliberate attention to students will result in the overly simplistic conclusion that students are simply poor decoders or poor comprehenders. In fact, purchasing, adopting, or designing an intervention without this kind of information would likely be a futile consumption of teacher energy, student time, and fiscal resources. Chapters 6 and 7 of this book more fully describe assessment systems and how they can be used instructionally.

Interventions Should Include Significant Opportunities for Authentic Reading and Writing

We do not know of any struggling readers who became better readers by *not* reading. Indeed, there is strong evidence to suggest that time spent reading separates good readers from poor readers (Allington, 2001). If teachers want low-achieving readers to look and act like successful readers, it stands to reason that any intervention ought to include many opportunities for students to actually read. In fact, it should be the focal point of the instructional time. Unfortunately, many struggling students are assigned to special reading programs in the elementary grades that focus on skill-and-drill activities to the exclusion of authentic reading and writing (Johnston & Allington, 1991).

Working on skills and strategies should facilitate real reading and writing, and this instruction should take place in the context where students actually need to know how to use them and have purposes for using them. Furthermore, the amount of time students spend reading and writing (truly *engaged* in reading and writing rather than reluctantly pulled through a difficult or uninteresting text by the teacher) ought to substantially outweigh the amount of time that students spend practicing skills and strategies related to literacy. As with Natalie at the beginning of this chapter, we ideally imagine a student spending a significant portion of the intervention time actively reading or writing.

Planning Intensive Interventions

Like all lessons, one-to-one intensive interventions require planning to make the most of instructional time and to prevent the session from devolving into a less pedagogically rigorous lesson that focuses on helping rather than teaching. Some of the same principles that apply to effective group teaching also apply to the individual lesson, such as activation of background knowledge, introduction of concepts and vocabulary, and student demonstration of learning. To plan an effective intensive intervention lesson, consider the following questions (Frey, 2006).

What is the purpose of the lesson? Teachers have known for decades that learners perform better when they understand the purpose of the lesson. Intensive intervention efforts are no different; the learner must understand the purpose. This therefore means that the teacher must also understand the purpose. Luckily, teachers today have a range of options. Some intensive intervention lessons are designed to match the student's *rate of learning*. By previewing skills, for example, the teacher can give the student who performs significantly below grade level an opportunity to catch up and participate in the core instruction. Another purpose is *content instruction* designed to ensure that the student has the factual or conceptual knowledge necessary to participate in core instruction. A third purpose may be to provide an alternative *method of presentation* so that the student can access content knowledge. Finally, one-to-one lessons may be conducted to teach *alternative learning goals* that are not taught to other members of the class, especially learning goals that rapidly build academic language skills so that the student can participate effectively in core instruction.

What are the student's background knowledge and prior experiences? For some students, the lack of prior experience and background knowledge is the main contributor to poor performance. For others, it's a contributing factor. Far too often, students require intensive intervention simply because they lack the background knowledge to understand the content (Fisher & Frey, 2009). Regardless, an intensive intervention lesson should be based on the unique academic and life experiences that a student has had, as well as the background knowledge that he or she possesses.

What are the targeted skills or strategies for this lesson? Given that intensive intervention sessions are academically demanding and last 20–40 minutes, teachers must resist the urge to cram too many skills or strategies into one session. In addition to causing unnecessary confusion, it's also exhausting and can result in fatigue that interferes with the remainder of the school day. It is better to focus on specific concepts or skills, teach them, and then return the student to the flow of core instruction and supplemental intervention. In other words, intensive intervention is about precision.

How will essential vocabulary be taught? Intensive intervention provides teachers with a great opportunity to introduce and practice academic vocabulary, both orally and in writing. A few minutes of instruction and discussion is useful for expanding vocabulary, which will help the student succeed in core instruction and in other reading experiences (Frey & Fisher, 2009).

What will the student produce? An important effectiveness measure of any lesson is the assessment of learning. Evidence of learning can assume a multitude of forms, including oral, written, and performance products. Effective intensive intervention lessons always have a product that is directly related to the learning goal, allows the teacher to check for understanding and plan the next lesson, and enables the student to practice academic language skills.

What future skills will the student need? Knowing what future skills the student will require is perhaps the most critical part of intensive intervention, because the primary goal of this type of support is to integrate core classroom instruction as much as possible. Integration can be a particular challenge when Tier 3 instruction is designed and delivered by a person other than the classroom teacher. Conflicting schedules can interfere with educators' good intentions, and, typically, the conversations that should occur somehow don't. That is why it is critical that a feedback loop be built into the structure of any RTI^2 effort. You may recall from Chapter 1 that Adam's classroom teacher and the reading specialist consulted regularly so that the reading specialist could select materials that were relevant to Adam's content learning. In addition, the school had a standing committee charged with analyzing qualitative and quantitative data on students in Tier 3 intervention in order to continuously make improvements to the school's quality core instruction. The committee also facilitated planning between grade levels so that future supports could be discussed and designed. None of this coordination occurs by itself; it takes purposeful planning to make sure that reading specialists and classroom teachers communicate with each other weekly (even if only by e-mail) to discuss students' progress. RTI^2 committees should hold monthly meetings with standing agendas that include points for discussion. Schools that anticipate students' future skills needs can avoid communicative and programmatic breakdowns that are otherwise inevitable.

Putting It All Together: Aligning Core, Supplemental, and Intensive Efforts

Raquel, a 7th grade student who reads far below grade level, has been in the United States since she was 6 years old. She has yet to be redesignated as fluent English proficient and has been identified as "intermediate" in her language proficiency for several years. She lives with her brother and his wife and has attended two middle schools and four elementary schools thus far in her schooling experience. Her current middle school has more than 1,200 students enrolled in grades 6–8. The school operates on a four-by-four block schedule with 90-minute classes. This term, Raquel has English/genre, science, English language development, and math. She attends an after-school program funded by the U.S. Department of Education. The first 90 minutes of the after-school program focus on tutoring and homework assistance, and the remaining two hours are set aside for social and recreational activities. Raquel regularly selects music and art for her post-tutoring activities.

As part of her after-school program, Raquel receives 20 to 30 minutes per day of individualized instruction from a credentialed teacher who has a master's degree in reading. In addition to this individualized instruction, she reads for 20 to 30 minutes and completes center activities and tasks with a small group of students for the remaining time. During the school day, Raquel participates in 15 minutes of sustained silent reading (SSR) each day and another 20 to 30 minutes of intensive intervention with a language development specialist. Raquel likes to read series books and is currently reading the fourth Lemony Snicket book. She talks with her classmates about these books and was overheard telling one that she practices the books at school so that she can read them at night to her brother and sisters.

In addition to her SSR time, a portion of Raquel's intervention time is devoted to independent reading. In both SSR and independent reading, students read books on their own. The difference between the two times is in the book selection. During SSR time, Raquel selects any reading material she wants. During independent reading, the teacher narrows the choice to texts that are at Raquel's independent reading level and that are based on the topics that Raquel is working on during her intervention. The books that Raquel reads during the after-school reading intervention program are often shorter and can be read in a single sitting. Looking through the bin of books that have been set aside for Raquel, it is easy to see that she enjoys music and art. The books include *Lives of the Artists*, *Lives of the Musicians*, *Frida*, *My Name Is Georgia*, and *When Marian Sang*. When asked about the number of books in her bin, Raquel commented, "I didn't know they had so many girl artists.... I didn't read books in my other school, only these papers the teacher gave us."

According to her intervention teacher, the center activities add to Raquel's understanding of language and focus on "the structure and function of the English language" as part of the school's focused English language development curriculum (Dutro & Moran, 2003). There are a number of centers in the room, including word sorts, listening stations with books read on CD, and grammar games. In a small group, Raquel and three other students each read different picture books with RAFT writing prompts written on the inside. RAFT writing prompts (Role, Audience, Format, Topic) help writers use perspective to write for different audiences (Santa & Havens, 1995). Raquel works on a RAFT prompt that is written inside the wordless picture book *You Can't Take a Balloon into the Metropolitan Museum*. It reads:

R — balloon
A — tourists
F — postcard
T — why you should visit the Metropolitan Museum

Raquel is hard at work, trying to fit her ideas into the space of a postcard; she rewrites her sentences to be as concise as possible.

During her individualized reading intervention, Raquel practices her part in a readers' theater script. Repeated readings, an integral part of the readers' theater experience, are an effective and purposeful means for building reading fluency (Worthy & Broaddus, 2001/2002). Raquel and a group of her classmates in the after-school program prepare a presentation of *Zin! Zin! Zin! A Violin* for the other students and teachers. In this rhyming picture book, 10 instruments are introduced one by one in a musical performance. The performance begins with one voice—the trombone—and an additional voice is added as each new instrument is described.

Raquel's teacher first reads the entire book aloud, modeling fluency and appropriate expression. Afterward, they talk about unfamiliar vocabulary (e.g., *valves*, *bleating*, *mournful*). Raquel and her teacher then take turns reading aloud, and finally, they read the book in unison. During each successive reading, Raquel's confidence and fluency improve.

As Raquel begins to practice her assigned part, her teacher notes some ways she can read the passage to make it more engaging and comprehensible to the audience. For example, she must read, "Now, a mellow friend, the cello, neck extended, bows a hello" (Moss, 1995, p. 7). In her initial reading, Raquel reads *cello* and *hello* with a similar intonation. Her teacher points out that it would be more effective to read *hello* as if she were actually using it in a conversational greeting, with an emphasis on the final *o*. Raquel agrees and incorporates this into her performance.

Obviously, the intervention support provided to Raquel required significant teacher involvement, from selecting texts, to modeling, to providing feedback, to gradually releasing responsibility for reading. Raquel received many opportunities for real reading and writing, and the texts used for instruction were clearly interesting and often connected by subject. Initial and ongoing assessments helped Raquel's teacher find materials that made sense to Raquel. Also, integral reading process components were addressed within the context of more substantial, purposeful, and connected reading and writing experiences (e.g., fluency practice was embedded within a readers' theater activity).

While it is likely that Raquel will require more explanations for and further teacher modeling of vocabulary, fluency, and comprehension within the context of reading and writing, her time after school is well spent. It is fairly easy to predict that Raquel will make great strides in literacy in terms of achievement and motivation because of the coordinated efforts of her teachers. The core instruction was of a high quality, and the supplemental and intensive interventions were designed around Raquel's specific needs. (Authors' note: Our prediction came true. Raquel now attends college and is majoring in social work. Her university grade point average stands at 3.79, a testament to the instruction she received in middle and high school.)

The Takeaway

After you have read this chapter, consider the following key points:

• Intensive intervention requires the specialized supports afforded through one-to-one instruction.

• One-to-one instruction increases academic intensity by providing the teacher with opportunities to customize instruction to meet the learning trajectory of individual students.

• Tier 3 interventions capitalize on increased intensity through access to expertise, specialized diagnostic assessments, augmented lesson frequency, and overall duration.

6

The Role of Assessment in RTI^2:

Progress Monitoring for Student Success

Marlon, a 7th grade student, is new to the district and has demonstrated reading difficulties since his arrival. He took a universal screening assessment in reading during the first week of school and scored at the 11th percentile compared to his same-age peers. Because of this low performance, his English teacher placed him in a small, needs-based group that met with her three times a week. In addition, the science and social studies teachers preview content with Marlon and discuss his responses on anticipation guides.

The school's fall benchmark assessment, the Analytic Reading Inventory, further confirms that he is reading well below grade level. The English teacher begins working with Marlon twice a week and gathers more assessment data, including curriculum-based measurements of oral reading fluency. A collaborative team, including Marlon's mother, meets regularly to discuss Marlon's progress. By the winter, Marlon makes some progress, but it is not enough to ensure his success. The reading specialist begins providing individual instruction to Marlon three times a week and collects detailed reading information, including his score on the Qualitative Reading Inventory, in order to further understand where his reading difficulties lay. The team continues to meet with Marlon's mother, sometimes over the telephone, to keep her apprised of Marlon's progress.

By spring, Marlon's lack of progress has become more significant. Despite classroom instruction and intervention, Marlon is not showing the desired gains. The RTI[2] committee meets to talk about next steps. The team draws on data from the numerous assessments that have been compiled over the course of the year. With Marlon's mother's consent, they refer Marlon for further special education assessment to determine eligibility. "In his other schools, it seemed like he just got passed over," Marlon's mother says. "He's a good kid, and quiet. I think they didn't take notice. I would have hoped he'd have done better this year, but I do appreciate that lots of folks took the time to work with him."

Purposes of Assessment

Assessments have long been a hallmark of the learning process because they can describe a student's present understanding and provide useful feedback to the teacher on what's working and what's not. Assessment has become even more important during the last century as increasingly sophisticated methods have come into vogue. The advent of intelligence testing before World War I gave rise to a host of measures that purported to differentiate entire segments of the population. Criticisms about the misuse of such tests to justify morally and ethically questionable practices led to a diminished reliance on tests for measuring nebulous qualities such as intelligence and aptitude. Although still in use today, such tests are now viewed as only one data point; it is necessary to take additional measures to achieve a richer portrait of a person.

So it is with our broader understanding of assessment. We understand that one measure alone could never do justice to a person or a program; we need to look through multiple lenses in order to get a good representation of areas of strength and need. Marlon's referral for special education testing came only after several people had gotten to know him as a learner over the course of a year and taken the time to document their work. As the appreciation of the relative strengths and limitations of assessments has developed, so has the ability to appropriately align instruments with purposes. In general, there are four broad purposes for assessment (Lapp, Fisher, Flood, & Cabello, 2000):

- progress monitoring
- diagnosis
- program evaluation
- accountability

The first three (progress monitoring, diagnosis, and program evaluation) are especially pertinent to any discussion of RTI^2. This is not to say that accountability doesn't play a role, but it is beyond the scope of this book to discuss issues regarding state and federal accountability measures. Assessment, however, is central to RTI^2 efforts. In fact, assessments drive the entire RTI^2 system!

Monitoring Student Progress

Knowing what you want to measure is one thing; knowing the tools available to do so is another. The types of assessments available are ultimately only as good as their suitability for performing an intended task. In other words, matching is key. Good assessments ultimately lose their value if they are misapplied. Therefore, a closer look at the types of assessments, as well as their purposes, is in order (see Figure 6.1).

Formal Assessments

Teachers and administrators are certainly familiar with the standardized and criterion-referenced tests that have become ubiquitous in schools. These are considered formal because they contribute to the formal measurements (outcomes) of a student's academic life, including grades and promotion. In addition, formal assessments typically undergo a more rigorous design process so that a student's performance can be compared against something—either a large population of other students (standardized) or an expected level or benchmark (criterion-referenced). Familiar standardized tests include TerraNova, the California Achievement Test-6 (CAT-6), and the Iowa Tests of Basic Skills (ITBS). Criterion-referenced tests often use standards as criteria and are familiar to teachers, families, and students. Examples include the Texas Essential Knowledge and Skills (TEKS) and the Michigan Educational Assessment Program (MEAP).

Curriculum-based measurements (CBMs) are a central feature of student progress monitoring and decision making about instruction and intervention. Sometimes called general outcome measures, CBMs can be either standardized or criterion-referenced, depending on whether the comparison made is to a population average or to a criterion. Criteria associated with early mathematics measures, for example, include number identification, quantity discrimination, and computational fluency. An online generator for such measures can be found at Intervention Central, a free Web site with resources for RTI measures (www.interventioncentral.org).

Figure 6.1
Formal and Informal Assessments Useful in RTI[2]

Formal Assessments		
Type	**Purpose**	**Administration**
Standardized	Yields a student's academic performance ranking compared to a normed sample of students.	Schedule is determined by state and local agencies, often yearly. Tests are usually timed and have strict protocols.
Criterion-referenced	Measures a student's performance against grade or age expectations in a set of academic skills or objectives. Scores are reported as the proportion of correct answers.	Tests may be untimed or timed. May be administered annually or more frequently.
Curriculum-based measurement	Allows for more finely tuned measurements of student progress toward grade or age expectations.	Administered frequently to compare progress and gauge effects of instruction and intervention.
Teacher-made and publisher-made tests (e.g., true/false, fill-in, multiple choice)	Measures retention and comprehension of specific content.	Administered within the lesson plan; students answer focused questions in various formats.

Informal Assessments		
Type	**Purpose**	**Administration**
Observation	Gathers information about a student's academic, behavioral, or social skills in an authentic setting.	Teacher records observational data in anecdotal notes, journals, or daily logs.
Checklist	Documents a student's use of specific skills during one or more observations.	A commercially or teacher-produced form of observable behaviors is completed by the teacher.
Rubric	Compares a student's work to a pre-established set of criteria that are scaled to guide student performance.	Teacher shares rubric with students, collects student work, and compares it to the rubric.
Self-assessment	Allows a student to engage in reflective learning and establish goals for future learning.	Students assess their own academic performance using an age-appropriate checklist of indicators.

When CBMs produce normative data, they also provide useful information to compare a student's progress against expected measures, offering a level of technical adequacy that informal measures do not offer. An excellent example of this principle can be found in the oral reading fluency norms for grades 1 to 8 (Hasbrouck & Tindal, 2006). These published norms include percentile rankings and administration data for fall, winter, and spring.

Another widely used CBM is the Dynamic Indicators of Basic Early Literacy Skills (DIBELS) (Good, Gruba, & Kaminski, 2002). This test is considered to be criterion-referenced because it is based on a set of indicators (criteria) associated with emergent literacy. In addition, national norms that indicate expected levels of achievement have been generated. DIBELS has proven to be popular in part because the results can be interpreted in both ways.

Teachers need not rely only on national norms established by other researchers; districts can establish local norms by compiling data on the performance of large groups of students, a process that Deno describes as being of particular usefulness to urban districts "where concerns exist regarding the degree to which the norms of commercially available standardized tests reflect the rapidly changing diversity of student populations" (2003, p. 187).

You may have noticed that many of the examples so far have been applicable to elementary-aged students, especially in reading. Research on curriculum-based measurements led by Stanley Deno and his colleagues at the University of Minnesota has been conducted for more than 20 years. However, for many years, this work was concentrated on the fields of early reading, writing, and spelling, so there is less in the literature about other content areas or applicability to secondary students. Curriculum at the middle and high school levels is further complicated by its complexity. It is simply a much bigger leap to make a connection between a constrained skill such as letter identification and an unconstrained skill such as comprehending a textbook passage about the causes and effects of the Glorious Revolution of 1688 (Paris, 2005).

Deno (2003) notes that many criteria used at the elementary level do not have the same strong statistical relationship that they do at the high school level. However, this is not to say that there are no curriculum-based measurements appropriate for high school. One promising line of research is in the development of a writing CBM for high school students. Christine Espin and her associates have found that analyzing a 7- to 10-minute writing sample using a formula to determine the ratio of correct to incorrect word sequences has a statistically high relevance to performance on state writing tests (Espin, Wallace, Lembke, Long, & Ticha, 2008). A correct word sequence is defined as "two adjacent correctly spelled words considered acceptable within the context of the sentence as judged by a native speaker" (p. 176). (A detailed scoring guide can be found at www.progressmonitoring.org/pdf/RIPM_Writng_Scoring.pdf.) This CBM appears to be valid for English language learners as well. While the researchers caution that more work needs to be done to firmly establish the technical adequacy of this measure, its usefulness at the high school level is evident. Given that writing has such strong relevancy across the curriculum, a writing CBM would be quite meaningful.

Many districts use measures such as the oral reading fluency norms, early mathematics indicators, and DIBELS as screening instruments to determine which students might need further intervention. This practice has not been without controversy, and critics have expressed concern over the use of superficial measures of reading or math behavior as a means of making significant educational decisions. We agree with Hasbrouck and Tindal, who point out that "the result of any screening measure must be viewed as one single piece of valuable information to be considered when making important decisions about a student, such as placement in an instructional program or possible referral for academic assistance" (2006, p. 640).

Keep in mind that the purpose of curriculum-based measurements is to provide the teacher and student with frequent and formative feedback on learning. By definition, these measures are typically quick to administer (less than 10 minutes) and are meant to gauge progress and determine the effectiveness of instruction and intervention. The criteria used for CBMs are skills-based, which can lead to the unintended practice of constricting instruction to discrete skills. CBMs should be employed in a fashion similar to the way a thermometer is used. Body temperature is an indicator of health, but taking a temperature is not the same as treating an illness. A high temperature is indicative of other problems, such as an infection, and although treatment might include lowering body temperature, it should also include a more comprehensive plan for locating the source of the infection and administering appropriate medicine. In the same way, a CBM indicating whether a child knows numbers or letters is informational, but it is not equivalent to instruction and intervention. A child who doesn't know his or her letters will benefit from opportunities to master them, but that child also needs opportunities to apply his or her growing letter knowledge by reading and writing about the surrounding world. A good instruction and intervention plan ensures that the child gets both.

Formal assessment measures, particularly curriculum-based measurements, provide information to teachers and families that is easily collected and analyzed. However, there is still a need for other forms of assessment information to capture a fuller picture of who the student is and how he or she is progressing. This is especially true at the secondary level, where fewer identified criteria can be readily measured using a CBM format. However, curriculum-based assessments, which are derived directly from the curriculum rather than from identified criteria, are useful for monitoring progress and informing instruction and intervention.

Teacher-made and publisher-made tests (those that accompany a specific textbook) are considered to be formal assessments in their administration. These are more frequently used in the classroom than the measures previously discussed, and they have merit as far as measuring retention and comprehension of their specific content. They are subject to a number of variables, including test construction and content instruction. However, they serve as part of a full portrait of a student's achievement, especially because they provide a snapshot of a student's progress in a moment in time.

Informal Assessments

Curriculum-based assessments (CBAs) focus attention on mastery learning of course curriculum. Like more formal CBMs, they are administered frequently to monitor student progress, provide useful formative feedback to the learner, and inform decisions about instruction and intervention. CBAs are often teacher-constructed samples of curriculum content derived from materials that the student is using, such as textbook passages, problem sets, and spelling lists. Because CBAs require direct observation of the student, it is helpful to have a range of tools available to collect performance data.

Observations. Watching students as they work in the classroom provides teachers with important information about students' knowledge, strategies, skills, and behaviors. Sometimes, these observations are conducted in natural settings, such as while students complete learning tasks or interact with peers. At other times, teachers specially construct an activity in order to observe a student's response. Regardless, teachers report that observations are one of the most important sources of information they have about students.

Yetta Goodman (1985) coined the term *kidwatching* to describe the observation prowess of teachers. One of the ways that teachers engage in kidwatching is by keeping anecdotal records—brief notes about a student. Observations can be conducted using a clipboard with sticky notes on which teachers jot quick sentences about a student's academic or social behavior. Later, these notes can be added to pages in a binder for more permanent recordkeeping. Some teachers transfer their observational notes to an electronic file for easy analysis. Over time, teachers can examine their anecdotal records for trends. Although teachers cannot possibly begin to document every observation, periodic documentation can assist teachers in planning lessons and sharing information with students, parents, administrators, and colleagues. Meeting with a student and his or her family to discuss classroom performance is often more productive when the teacher has examples of that performance to share.

For example, during a parent conference, Ms. Thompson notes that Jessica, a 6th grade student, regularly (four out of five times) starts writing as soon as a prompt is given but rarely (one out of five times) completes the task. In addition to observing Jessica's natural behavior, her teacher creates a task specifically to allow her to observe Jessica and record her responses. Ms. Thompson meets with Jessica a few days after the parent meeting and says, "Remember our conversation with your mom the other day? You said that you would like to be a better writer, which I know you can do. How about we take some time while the groups are working and you talk out loud while you respond to today's prompt. I'll take notes about what you say and what you write so that we can talk further about your becoming the amazing writer you want to be." Jessica agrees and talks out loud as she writes. Ms. Thompson takes notes for later analysis. Over several observations, Ms. Thompson realizes that Jessica is losing her train of thought because she immediately starts writing and doesn't have a plan. This, then, becomes the focus of Jessica's instruction.

Checklists. Checklists can also be helpful tools for documentation because they allow teachers to specify particular dimensions for observation, and they provide a means for summarizing those observations. Teachers may use a checklist as a simple instrument for capturing students' evolving skills. For example, a math checklist was developed by teachers in the

Pequea Valley School District in Pennsylvania to assess students' understanding and to track instruction and intervention. Sample items from grade 3 included

- Distinguishes between odd and even numbers.
- Identifies place value through thousands.
- Rounds whole numbers to the nearest ten, hundred, or thousand (no greater than 9,000).
- Compares two whole numbers using >, <, and = through 9,999.

Just imagine the conversations that this tool could facilitate between the classroom teacher and supplemental and intensive intervention teachers, as well as between the classroom teacher and family members. When checklists are used in this manner, they become a critical component of the assessment system from which teachers can draw to effectively implement RTI^2.

Rubrics. Rubrics are often used as an assessment tool because they provide teachers and students with a definition of quality work. Using rubrics, students will likely understand the important elements on which they will be evaluated. Rubrics provide students with criteria for each level of achievement and can be used to determine needed instruction as well as mastered content. (They can also be used to facilitate grading, but that function is beyond the scope of this book.) While development of the rubric is critical, teaching students how to use a rubric and understand its criteria is even more important. Rubistar (http://rubistar.4teachers.org) is a free Web site that helps teachers create and share rubrics.

Self-assessments. In many classrooms, the teacher is the primary evaluator. On those infrequent occasions when students participate in the assessment process, their involvement is nominal; for example, students might check a classmate's work against answers written on the board. Far rarer is the classroom where students are asked to identify their own goals and monitor their progress toward those goals. An exclusive reliance on externally driven assessment systems can have a negative effect on students' achievement and attitude toward learning (Johnston & Winograd, 1985; Winograd & Paris, 1989). The use of self-assessment not only supports student learning but also can serve as a student motivator.

Several promising developments suggest greater student involvement in planning and progress monitoring. An example of such a development is the emphasis during the 1990s on brain-based learning. Neurobiologists have shown that the search for meaning is innate and that meaning emanates from the learner, not the teacher (Diamond & Hopson, 1998). The regular use of self-assessment increases each learner's ability to seek and identify goals that are personally meaningful. In addition, the data collected via student self-assessments are useful in planning instruction and intervention.

In some cases, self-assessment is used over the course of a project. Students plan and reflect at the beginning, middle, and end of the project. Self-assessment then becomes part of the project itself. Students who are taught to plan and monitor their work habits begin to take ownership of their work.

Assessing one's abilities and setting goals is an important aspect of learning. This element deserves increased attention in RTI^2 efforts because there are indications that emphasizing metacognition can create opportunities for students to achieve at higher levels by promoting cognitive and affective development (Heritage, 2009; Soldner, 1997).

You've Collected the Data—Now What?

We've always liked the old saying that cautions, "You can't fatten sheep by weighing them." In the same way, you can't teach children by assessing them, any more than a doctor can cure a patient simply by repeatedly taking his or her temperature. Data collection is useful only if the next step is data analysis. However, the task of manipulating all that data can be intimidating. With this in mind, we've added another piece of advice to that maxim: "You also can't fatten sheep if you're too busy to feed them."

As we explained in Chapter 2, a purposeful look at student progress includes progress monitoring and decision making. The data collected and analyzed should result in improved education experiences for the individual student and feed back into communities of practice that focus on continuous school improvement. The data collected and analyzed, especially within the core curriculum, should also be set up as an early warning system to catch learners who are beginning to fall behind their peers. As with other aspects of RTI^2, assessment and data analysis intensity is proportional to time and access to expertise.

Intensifying Assessment Through Time and Expertise

Any worthwhile early-warning system is predicated on collecting and analyzing data early and often. So it is with RTI^2. The first level of assessment is screening, followed by benchmark assessments, which are then intensified by curriculum-based measurements and assessments that can provide more specialized information. Each of these levels also presents opportunities for collaboration among distinct areas of expertise.

Universal Screening

Schoolwide screening, sometimes called universal screening, is designed to assist the teacher in getting an initial sense of which students might need extra help acquiring skills and content. Classroom-based screening ranges from the readiness assessments common in kindergarten (e.g., writing one's name and drawing a simple self-portrait) to sample math problems given to every high school student during the first week of classes. Examining screening results can provide immediate valuable information. For instance, at some schools, the lowest-scoring 20 percent of students may receive additional small-group instruction in the classroom from the beginning of the school year. In other cases, the screening may be more formal. Many California high school students take a 45-item mathematics readiness test designed by the Mathematics Diagnostic Testing Project (MDTP), a collaborative program of the California State University and University of California systems. The results are scored and compiled by MDTP as a free service to California schools. (More information about these materials can be found at http://mdtp.ucsd.edu.)

Universal screenings also provide an opportunity for collaboration across grade levels and departments, as well as with families. General and special educators assigned to a grade level or a department can examine and discuss the results in order to make decisions about grouping. Staffing decisions about the use of paraprofessional time can be scheduled based on the level of need in each room, rather than on a simplistic model composed of even units of time. In addition, the results of the screening can be shared with the family so that conversations about student progress can begin long before the first report card is sent home.

Progress Monitoring

Sometimes the same instruments used for initial screening may be administered multiple times a year to monitor progress. For example, reading fluency measurements may be gathered and analyzed in the fall, winter, and spring to evaluate an individual student's progress. Expected progress levels can be identified through national norming, such as DIBELS, or through local norming, such as district-specific benchmarks. Lack of progress along the expected trajectory would trigger further instruction and intervention, as described throughout this book.

Benchmark assessments provide another opportunity for collaboration within the school. In one district we work with, literacy coaches assist teachers in administering the Developmental Reading Assessment (Beavers, 1999), an informal reading inventory that is administered individually. This collaboration gives coaches an opportunity to consult with teachers about students who are showing early signs of falling behind. In a high school we work with, the mathematics department chair brings the results of each benchmark assessment cycle to her meetings with teachers. "I have several newer teachers in my department," she said. "We look at the results together and develop a plan for at-risk students. It's a great way to discuss instructional practice while building their ability to use assessment data constructively."

Checking for Mastery

Students who participate in Tier 2 and Tier 3 interventions are assessed more frequently in order to gauge the effectiveness of instruction. These measures include CBMs and CBAs developed by teachers to assess learning mastery. The consultative services of special educators are especially useful for this. In many cases, members of the special education department provide professional development and follow up by familiarizing general educators with curriculum-based measurements and developing their own curriculum-based assessments. "We had never heard of CBAs until a few years ago," remarked a 7th grade English teacher. "Fortunately, Ms. Durant [the special educator for her grade level] told us she had first learned about it in her credential program. She taught us all how to do it."

Diagnostics

There are students who participate in high-quality core instruction and intervention but still do not make progress. In those cases, assessment is further intensified through the use of measures that yield diagnostic information. Examples include formal testing by special education teachers, such as the Woodcock Reading Mastery Tests; by speech-language pathologists, such as the Peabody Picture Vocabulary Test; or by the school psychologist, such as the Wechsler Intelligence Scale for Children.

Clear guidance about how diagnostic assessments should be used is extremely valuable. Call it "assessing the assessments," if you like. We believe that the system used by the Heartland Area Education Agency in Iowa and described by Hosp (2006) accomplishes exactly this. Heartland employs a decision-making rubric called RIOT/ICEL to structure their diagnostic assessment system and make sure that relevant information is not overlooked (see Figure 6.2). This process also helps to ensure that irrelevant information is not included. One axis of this matrix describes the process:

- **R**eview records and any existing documents, including evidence of prior interventions.
- **I**nterview teachers, family members, and other personnel who have knowledge of the student and his or her performance.
- **O**bserve the child within and outside of the classroom.
- **T**est using carefully matched assessment instruments.

The other axis of the matrix describes the relevant educational domains:

- **I**nstruction, including grouping arrangements, task demands, and opportunities for scaffolding.
- **C**urriculum, especially the content and its pacing.
- **E**nvironment, such as the physical and social aspects of the classroom.
- **L**earner factors that might affect performance, such as health and well-being.

Although the RIOT/ICEL matrix was designed with school psychologists in mind, we believe this method of inquiry is useful for all educators, including classroom teachers and communities of practice, such as the RTI[2] committee.

Figure 6.2
RIOT/ICEL Assessment Matrix

	Review	Interview	Observe	Test
Instruction	*Review Instruction*	Interview those who know about instruction	*Observe instruction*	Test instruction
Curriculum	*Review the Curriculum*	Interview those who know about the curriculum	*Observe the curriculum*	Test the curriculum
Environment	*Review the Environment*	Interview those who know about the environment	*Observe the environment*	Test the environment
Learner	*Review the Learner*	Interview those who know about the learner	*Observe the learner*	Test the learner

Source: Heartland Area Education Agency 11, Johnson, Iowa. Used with permission.

Analyzing Assessment Data

Recognizing the expected criteria-based outcomes, such as oral reading fluency, or curriculum-based outcomes, such as mastery of integers, is vital to data analysis. After all, you have to know where you're going in order to get a bearing on where you are. Therefore, data analysis, as described initially in Chapter 2, is about performing a gap analysis of where a student is and where he or she should be, and then monitoring progress toward that objective. One of the easiest ways to make these trajectories meaningful to fellow educators, students, and families is to chart their progress. Visual displays of information are helpful to determine whether instruction and intervention are effective or in need of refinement.

The chief purpose of charting and graphing student progress is to examine trend lines and see if sufficient advancement toward mastery is occurring. If the trend line does not appear to be moving at a satisfactory rate, then the methods of instruction and intervention need to be examined for possible improvements. A collaborative conversation—between a classroom teacher and a peer coach or between a classroom teacher and a consulting special educator, for example—should result in adjustments to curriculum and instruction. These visual displays also serve as a means for the RTI[2] committee to discuss how core instruction can be refined to better support student learning.

The graph in Figure 6.3 illustrates the results of instruction and intervention that occurred over a 30-week period for Christopher, a 5th grade student whose inability to calculate multiplication facts fluently and accurately was undermining his ability to perform at grade level. Mr. Robertson, his classroom teacher, had noticed during the first weeks of school that Christopher's arithmetic errors explained many of the incorrect responses he had in his math assignments. Mr. Robertson's universal screening for math fluency confirmed his suspicions—Christopher was scoring well below expected levels for multiplication facts. The baseline data collected showed that he averaged only 14 correct responses out of a possible 50. Mr. Robertson increased the time Christopher spent on multiplication practice, using computerized multiplication drills in class. Mr. Robertson also began to collect data on Christopher's gains on a weekly basis. For several weeks, Christopher's performance hovered around 15 correct out of 50, indicating that extra time with the computer games was not helping much.

Mr. Robertson consulted with his 5th grade team, including the special educator for the grade level, about Christopher's lack of progress. They agreed that it was time to create Tier 2 supplemental interventions for Christopher. For the next 20 weeks, teacher and student worked on a host of drills, including flashcards and other games, to increase Christopher's multiplication fluency. Each week, he completed a one-minute drill, and Mr. Robertson charted the results. Christopher and his family were pleased with the weekly reports that Mr. Robertson shared with them, and their encouragement was motivating to Christopher. The trend line suggested steady progress during this period, and Mr. Robertson expanded his instruction and intervention to include reinforcement of the communicative property to increase Christopher's mathematical understanding of these facts and to build his capacity to memorize these functions. Mr. Robertson introduced arithmetic tables to further capitalize on Christopher's strengths as a visual learner. By the end of the school year, Christopher's math grades had improved significantly. "I don't get all nervous when I see word problems anymore," Christopher said. "I can solve them easy, 'cause I don't have to think too hard about my math facts. I can pay attention to solving the problem."

Based on the reports from Mr. Robertson and other 5th grade teachers with similarly achieving students, the team agreed that math fact practice

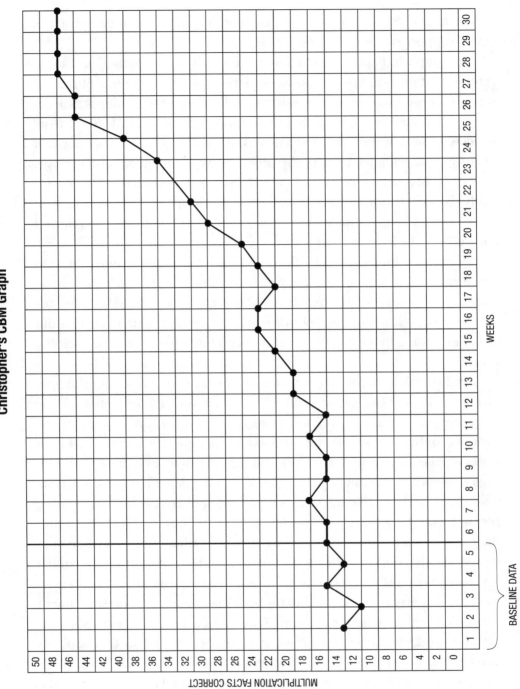

Figure 6.3
Christopher's CBM Graph

should be incorporated into daily math warm-ups. The team developed a simple format for reinforcing and practicing math fluency at the beginning of each lesson. "Lots of 5th graders don't have the math fluency they really should have to do more advanced math, so they get bogged down in the computations, which doesn't leave them with enough 'brain space' to pay attention to the mathematical concepts," Mr. Robertson explained. "If we can equip them for middle school math with a firm handle on math facts, we'll significantly affect their future achievement. Plus, the middle school folks will love us," he said with a smile.

The Takeaway

Check your own understanding of the key points from this chapter:

• Assessment and data analysis are critical to the RTI^2 process. Without this component, instruction and intervention are left to chance.

• Formal assessments provide normative data to compare student performance to expected levels. These comparisons can be to a national group or to a local one.

• Curriculum-based measurements are a critical feature of RTI^2. Although the approach has been around for decades, its application for analyzing responses to instruction and intervention for students without disabilities allows for a degree of precision and adjustment to teaching not commonly used in general education classrooms.

• Curriculum-based assessments are teacher-designed and draw upon more informal assessment measures. Student performance is compared to curriculum mastery.

• Data analysis should always result in examination of instruction and the curriculum. Visual displays of data are especially useful for holding collaborative conversations with colleagues, the family, and the student.

7

Feed-Up, Feedback, and Feed-Forward:

Progress Monitoring in Action

Much like Coleridge's ancient Mariner who says, "Water, water everywhere," teachers are awash with resources that sometimes aren't as helpful as might be expected. Most schools and districts have more assessment data than ever before. There is more information about individual students at teachers' fingertips than could be imagined a decade ago. We observed one teacher collecting literacy assessment data on her iPhone that was then synched to a computer program. It was impressive to see how quickly information about the students' reading skills was collected and stored. Unfortunately, when asked how she would use this information, the teacher replied, "It's just a benchmark test I'm required to give; I don't really use the info." Therein lies the problem: a resource that could significantly improve teaching and learning is rendered unusable.

The solution is twofold. First, we have to understand the components of a feedback system that improves both teaching and learning. Second, we have to align the multiple measures that are available to us and create a system of data collection, analysis, and impact that results in higher levels of student achievement.

Creating a Feedback System to Monitor Progress

Feedback as a construct is a powerful way to boost student achievement when it is done correctly (Hattie & Timperley, 2007). Meta-analyses on feedback consistently suggest that it is among the most powerful interventions teachers have at their disposal (Kluger & DeNisi, 1996). Some of the most effective components of feedback include providing cues to the learner; using video-, audio-, or computer-assisted mechanisms; and relating feedback to specific goals or objectives. Less effective components of feedback include general praise and/or punishment, but feedback is a complex construct with at least three distinct components. Fully implementing a feedback system requires that teachers use all three components, which we designate as feed-up, feedback, and feed-forward.

Feed-Up: Clarifying the Goal

The first component of a comprehensive feedback system involves purpose. When students understand the goal of the instruction, they are more likely to focus on the learning tasks at hand. When the goal "is clear, when high commitment is secured for it, and when belief in eventual success is high," student effort is amplified and achievement increases (Kluger & DeNisi, 1996, p. 260). The idea of having a purpose isn't new, but it is critical to the implementation of a feedback system, because when teachers exhibit a clear purpose, assessments can be aligned with that goal (Locke & Latham, 1990). For example, when an established purpose relates to comparing and contrasting the characteristics of insects and arthropods, students know what to expect in the lesson, and the teacher can plan instructional events such as shared readings, collaborative learning, and investigations to ensure that students focus their attention on this content. Similarly, when the established purpose is to persuade a reader using argumentation and facts, students have a clear sense of what is expected, and the teacher can plan instruction.

Feedback: Responding to Student Work

The second component, and the one that is more commonly recognized, relates to the individual responses to student work given by teachers. Of course, these responses should be directly related to the purpose and performance goal. The best feedback provides students with information about their progress or success and explains what course of action they can take to improve their understanding to meet the expected standard (Brookhart, 2008). Ideally, feedback occurs as students complete tasks so that they can continue to master content. If learning is the goal, teachers should not limit feedback to a summative review but rather provide formative feedback that students can use to improve their performance.

For example, in a unit of study on writing high-quality introductions, a teacher provides students with multiple opportunities to introduce topics using various techniques such as humor, questions, startling statistics, and direct quotations. For each introduction, the teacher provides feedback using a rubric so that students can revise their introductions and use that information on their next attempt. Rather than simply note mechanical errors that students make, the teacher acknowledges areas of success and provides recommendations for where students should focus their efforts in their next drafts.

Feed-Forward: Modifying Instruction

The final component required for creating a feedback system involves the use of data to plan instruction. Feed-forward systems involve greater flexibility in lesson planning, because teachers can't simply follow a script or implement a series of lesson plans that are carved in stone. This is the formative aspect of feedback, and it is one that is often missing. Student work, whether a daily check-for-understanding task or a common formative assessment tool, gives us information we can use to plan instruction. For example, students in one 3rd grade class complete a collaborative poster in response to a word problem that reads: "Six students are sitting at each table in the lunchroom. There are 23 tables. How many students are in the lunchroom?" The students in the class are supposed to answer the question using words, numbers, and pictures. However, nearly every group arrives at the wrong answer. Given this information, the teacher knows that she needs to provide more modeling for her students about how to solve word problems. The feed-forward, in this case, requires a whole-class reteaching intervention.

In one 5th grade classroom, the teacher notes that six students regularly capitalize random words in their writing assignments. Mauricio, for example, incorrectly capitalizes the words *fun*, *very*, *excited*, and *challenge* in his first paragraph. Given that the rest of the class is not making this type of error, the teacher knows that a feed-forward instructional intervention with the whole class is not necessary. Instead, he needs to provide additional guided instruction for the students who consistently make this type of error.

What Happens When Feedback Is Limited?

Without a feed-forward system that uses student responses to plan instruction, feedback may only increase students' need for supplemental and intensive intervention. In other words, if teachers provide students with feedback only, they are making an assumption that the learner understands the content of the feedback and can apply this knowledge to new situations. This approach works for some students, assuming that the feed-up purpose was understood, but it doesn't work for all students.

Consider Victor and the paper he submitted to his teacher (see Figure 7.1). Let's assume that Victor understood the purpose, which was to write a letter to the teacher discussing the book he was reading. The structure of these weekly literacy letters has been described elsewhere (Frey, Fisher, & Moore, 2009), but briefly, the first paragraph provides an update to the reader about the selected book and includes personal connections. The second paragraph is based on a prompt that is derived from the course content for the week, and it typically relates to state standards. The prompt in this particular case invited students to make a connection between the characters in the book and the essay they had submitted the previous week, which focused on the question "What sustains us?"

If Victor had received only the written feedback provided by the teacher on the letter, he probably wouldn't have been able to use it the following week. Feedback by itself places the entire responsibility for learning on the student. In doing so, the teacher violates the entire construct on which RTI^2 was built, namely, that assessment drives instruction and decisions about intervention.

Victor's teacher wrote, "Pay attention to possessives. Apostrophes are needed here." It isn't likely that Victor would be able to use this feedback, by itself, to use apostrophes correctly in the future. He wrote the paper as well as he knew how at the time, and without additional instruction, he's not likely to write any better next time.

Victor, however, was lucky because his teacher understood RTI^2. She had been working on writing mechanics with the whole class and noticed that there were several students, including Victor, who required additional instruction. To address this need, she planned to meet with Victor and the other students in a small group for guided instruction as part of her

Figure 7.1
Victor's Literacy Letter

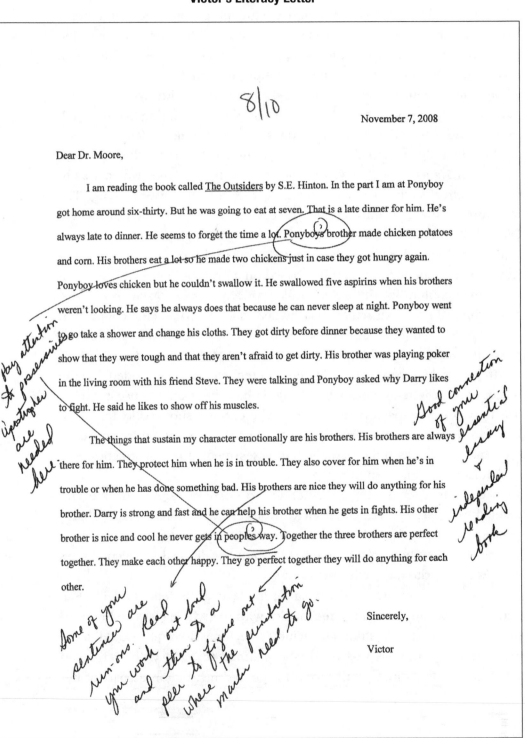

8/10

November 7, 2008

Dear Dr. Moore,

I am reading the book called <u>The Outsiders</u> by S.E. Hinton. In the part I am at Ponyboy got home around six-thirty. But he was going to eat at seven. That is a late dinner for him. He's always late to dinner. He seems to forget the time a lot. Ponyboys brother made chicken potatoes and corn. His brothers eat a lot so he made two chickens just in case they got hungry again. Ponyboy loves chicken but he couldn't swallow it. He swallowed five aspirins when his brothers weren't looking. He says he always does that because he can never sleep at night. Ponyboy went to go take a shower and change his cloths. They got dirty before dinner because they wanted to show that they were tough and that they aren't afraid to get dirty. His brother was playing poker in the living room with his friend Steve. They were talking and Ponyboy asked why Darry likes to fight. He said he likes to show off his muscles.

The things that sustain my character emotionally are his brothers. His brothers are always there for him. They protect him when he is in trouble. They also cover for him when he's in trouble or when he has done something bad. His brothers are nice they will do anything for his brother. Darry is strong and fast and he can help his brother when he gets in fights. His other brother is nice and cool he never gets in peoples way. Together the three brothers are perfect together. They make each other happy. They go perfect together they will do anything for each other.

Sincerely,

Victor

[Handwritten annotations: "Pay attention to possessives apostrophes are needed here"; "Good connection of your essential literacy → independent reading book"; "Some of your sentences are run-ons. Read out loud. You work out to a peer to figure out where the punctuation marks need to go."]

quality core instruction. If Victor (or any of the other students, for that matter) did not respond to this instruction, she would add supplemental instruction.

The teacher also wrote to Victor, "Some of your sentences are run-ons. Read your work out loud and then to a peer to figure out where the punctuation marks need to go." This is good advice that will mobilize peers in service of providing support. Having said that, if Victor continues to make errors with run-on sentences, his teacher will provide supplemental instruction and may ask one of the reading specialists to spend extra time with him.

Finally, Victor's teacher wrote, "Good connection of your essential essay & independent reading book." Clearly, Victor met the established purpose and demonstrated his thinking appropriately. By naming the specific aspect of his writing that was on target, his teacher provided him with reinforcement and gave him the sense that he is a successful writer.

Progress Monitoring Isn't Limited to Student-Level Data

In order for assessments to be informative, they must align with one another to present a rich portrait of student performance. For this reason, daily comprehension checks should contribute to the teacher's knowledge of how students will perform throughout a unit, in a course, and on state assessments. Daily checking for understanding should be linked to benchmark assessments (common formative assessments), competencies, and state assessments. Together, these form a nested system of assessment experiences that allow for feed-up, feedback, and feed-forward. This nested system is a requirement for sophisticated RTI^2 initiatives because it allows for actions to be taken at the individual student, classroom, and school levels.

Daily Checking for Understanding

At the core of the daily teaching event is the ability to check for understanding in a way that not only measures but also *informs*. At the heart of these practices are the ways we foster oral language and use questioning techniques (Fisher & Frey, 2007a). There is compelling evidence that points to the success of student talk as a mechanism for learning. The consensus is that classrooms with higher rates and levels of student talk excel academically (Stichter, Stormont, & Lewis, 2009).

Language frames are one system for developing higher rates and levels of academic talk in the classroom, and they serve as a way to check student understanding of concepts. Language frames are cloze-type statements that provide students with the academic language necessary to explain, justify, clarify, and ask for evidence. For example, 1st grade English language learners in mathematics are introduced to the language frame "The _____ is _____ than the _____" to contrast relative size between two objects. The teacher explains that the purpose of this lesson is to use this language frame to explain the size attributes of various animals to a partner (*feed-up*). When Joseph says, "The duck is narrower than the frog," his partner, Mario, then questions him, "Is the duck wider or narrower than the frog?" The math teacher then asks the boys to approximate the size of each animal for comparison (*feedback*). She sees that Joseph can perform the gestural task correctly, but he cannot accurately convert it to spoken language. Understanding that the barrier is language—and not the mathematical concept—she concentrates on reteaching the language frame until Joseph can use it correctly (*feed-forward*).

The use of questioning in the classroom is vital to checking for understanding, especially as it pertains to following up incorrect responses (*feedback*). When faced with a student error, teachers should remind themselves that the answer likely makes sense to the student *based on what he or she knows at that moment*. Therefore, our task as teachers is to rapidly form a hypothesis on what that knowledge might entail in order to provide the next prompt (*feed-forward*). Walsh and Sattes (2005) advise that follow-up prompts can include

• Words or phrases to foster recall. ("Think about the role of hydrogen…")

• Overt reminders to access memory. ("The word begins with the letter *d*.")

• Probes to elicit rationale in order to identify knowledge gaps. ("What led you to think the character would do that?")

• A rephrasing of the question to reduce language demands. ("Identify the role of tectonic plates in Earth's geophysical systems" can be rephrased as, "Earthquakes and volcanoes have at least one thing in common. Let's talk about that.")

• A recheck later in the lesson to see if the student has achieved comprehension. ("Now that we've learned a lot more, do you understand… now?")

Common Formative Assessments

In addition to the daily practice of checking for understanding, an aligned system also includes common formative assessments that allow teachers to effectively communicate and share results across grade levels or departments. These assessments are usually based on units of instruction and become part of the course's pacing guide. They serve as benchmarks to gauge smaller increments of student performance and provide teachers with data that spur conversation about instructional and curricular design. They also trigger conversations about students who need supplemental or intensive instruction. We recommend that teachers meet in advance of the unit to develop their own common formative assessment, as it encourages a focus on essential learning. The selected items, whether they are multiple choice, short answer, or essay, should serve a diagnostic purpose so that teachers can discuss misconceptions still held after instruction and recognize patterns among students. After the assessment is administered and scored, teachers should meet as soon as possible (that day or within a few days) to discuss the relationship between the results and the instruction that took place, as well as to plan the next instructional steps for students who need them.

Partial conceptual understanding is a common cause of incorrect responses. Witness an exchange between an English as a second language teacher and a student named Omar. The common formative assessment for which they are preparing focuses on affixes. The teacher explains that the purpose for the lesson is to structurally analyze new vocabulary words in small groups to determine what the students already know (*feed-up*). Omar incorrectly identifies *in-* as the prefix in *interlude*. Rather than simply supply him with the correct answer and then move on, the teacher first asks Omar what *in-* means and receives a correct reply. Omar then correctly identifies the meaning of *inter-*. The teacher asks, "Could the root be *-lude*, or is it *-terlude*?" Omar sticks with his initial incorrect answer, so the teacher tries again. She asks the group, "Is the prefix *in-* or *inter-*? That's all I'm going to say. I'll let you figure it out" (*feedback*). With the hint that his answer might not be correct, Omar talks with the members of his group about the two meanings and how they would affect the overall word. Importantly, the teacher returns to Omar several minutes later to check whether he and his group have arrived at the correct answer. By remembering to hold him accountable after further group discussion, she is able to check that Omar's understanding has progressed (*feed-forward*).

A few weeks later, after a common formative assessment is administered and scored, the teacher remarks during a department discussion, "I noticed some students in my class getting similar prefixes mixed up, such as *in-* and *inter-*. It looks like this is a pattern across all of our classes. How can we teach these two prefixes more effectively?" The teachers then engage in a conversation about learning theory, grammar, and linguistics, and they decide to develop a *Jeopardy!*-style game for students that includes easily confused affixes (*feed-forward*). In this way, common formative assessment results couple with daily checking-for-understanding experience and lead to a change in curriculum design.

As part of our work on RTI[2], we developed and refined a process to look at student work collaboratively and use assessment information to guide our next instructional steps (Fisher, Grant, Frey, & Johnson, 2007). We learned a lot from the work of Langer, Colton, and Goff (2003), but rather than provide common formative assessments as an option for teachers who want to use them, RTI[2] requires that this process be implemented schoolwide. We'll explain the four steps we use in common formative assessments and then provide examples of their use.

Step 1: Establish pacing guides. As an essential beginning point, groups of teachers who teach the same course (e.g., 3rd grade, Algebra I, U.S. History, 6th grade science, Biology) meet and agree on pacing guides. Pacing guides collectively identify when specific content standards will be taught, which instructional materials will be used, and which instructional strategies will be deployed. In addition to these components, pacing guides should indicate key vocabulary terms that are required for understanding, formative and summative assessments used to determine student understanding, accommodations that may be necessary for students with disabilities, universal access strategies for English language learners, and modifications for students who perform above grade level. A sample pacing guide format is shown in Figure 7.2.

Step 2: Create formative assessments. In addition to the pacing guides that contain summative assessments, teachers in their course-alike groups design, develop, or modify assessment items that are subsequently administered to all students, regardless of which teacher they have. Specific test items are developed to provide information that will help the teachers determine what students are understanding, where there are gaps in comprehension, and who needs intervention. As groups of teachers develop

Figure 7.2
Sample Pacing Guide Format

Course: _____   Unit of Study: _____   Essential Question: _____

Content Standards	Instructional Routines	Assessments	Suggested Texts/Time

Vocabulary Development (Target and Concept Vocabulary):

Accommodations and Modifications for English Language Learners, Above-Level Students, and/or Students with Disabilities:

these assessment items, they learn more about the content standards and how those standards might be assessed on state tests. In addition, they plan distractor items that will identify when students overgeneralize, oversimplify, or exhibit common misunderstandings about the content. A number of the common formative assessment items should mirror the state test design since test format practice is critical. Students must understand tests as a genre—how they work and what to expect. However, do not limit the items to those that emulate the state test; include short-answer, timed essays, constructed-response, and alternative-response items. There are a number of ways to determine students' understanding; the key to using formative assessments schoolwide is to determine the appropriate instructional "next steps," based on the results.

Step 3: Perform an item analysis. The third step occurs after a group of students has participated in the common formative assessment. In course-alike groups, teachers meet to discuss the results. It might be easiest to use a software program that provides an item analysis that indicates the percentage of students who selected each distractor. There are several commercially available software programs that do this well. Item analysis is key, as it allows teachers to look across the student body for trends—material that needs to be retaught, assessment items that need to be changed, or pacing guides that need to be revised. These computer programs also allow for a targeted examination of clusters of students. For example, it is possible to analyze how English language learners performed on a specific item. Item analysis provides a strong underpinning for instructional conversation and intervention.

Step 4: Engage in instructional conversation. The instructional conversation is why we do all of this work. Talking with colleagues who teach the same content and who see the same data results is foundational to instituting instructional improvements. In course-alike groups, teachers can determine which instructional strategies are working, which instructional materials are effective, and which students still need help to master the standards. As is evidenced in the examples that follow, instructional conversations allow teachers to return to their individual classrooms and engage in the real work of formative assessments—to reteach and intervene when students don't perform well.

Examining Student Work and Making Instructional Decisions

Ms. Grant is a science teacher who regularly facilitates conversations with her colleagues about student work. The students in her school recently took a biology common formative assessment. Afterward, the teachers in the science department discussed the student responses to the item shown in Figure 7.3.

Mr. Simms reported encouragingly, "The greatest percentage of students did choose the correct answer." Ms. Jackson quickly curbed the group's enthusiasm by noting, "But 54 percent of the students didn't choose the right answer." She added, "Seventeen percent chose answer A. This might mean that students don't understand how to determine percentages. I think that we should all do a quick review of some basic skills. Who can develop a quick review for us all to use?"

Mr. Simms offered to develop the review and then added, "I covered the main concepts of Mendelian genetics, but it seems that students didn't really understand how expressed traits are passed from parent to offspring." Mrs. Rodriguez agreed, "Yes, and 11 percent chose answer B. The students that chose this answer don't seem to understand the concept of a dominant allele. Maybe I need to focus more on vocabulary instruction for

Figure 7.3
Sample Biology Question and Results

In a certain species of insect, the allele for brown eyes (B) is dominant to the allele for blue eyes (b). For this species, eye color does not depend on the sex of the organism. When a team of scientists decided to cross a male and a female that both had brown eyes, they found that 31 offspring had brown eyes and 9 had blue eyes. What are the most likely genotypes of the parent insects?

A. BB and bb
B. bb and bb
C. Bb and Bb
D. BB and Bb

The percentage of students who chose each answer:

A. 17%
B. 11%
C. 46% (correct answer)
D. 26%

this group of students. We covered the key terms, but they don't seem to know how to use them. In addition to the math review, I think we should find out the specific students who missed this and get to them during small-group time."

Ms. Jackson also noted, "I think we need to work on test-taking skills. Our students should have been able to eliminate answers A and B right away because each shows a parent with blue eyes, and the question states that both parents have brown eyes." Mr. Simms added, "Twenty-six percent of our students chose answer D. Maybe they thought that since three out of four alleles are B, there's a correlation to the 31 out of 40 total insects with brown eyes as described in the question. I think I need to review how to use Punnett squares."

Ms. Grant wondered if the group thought that sharing the item analysis with students might also facilitate students' thinking about the content. She asked, "What if we showed all of the students this item analysis and asked them to work in small groups to determine why specific answers were wrong? Wouldn't that help them understand the test as a genre and get them test format practice?" Mr. Simms agreed, noting that this would also be teaching biology and not simply test practice. The teachers agreed to follow up with students and meet to discuss their progress later in the unit.

Mrs. Johnson is a teacher and the facilitator of the course-alike conversations in history. Like the science department, the history teachers use a common formative assessment to check students' understanding and determine which students need reteaching, intervention, or acceleration. The history department has piloted a metacognitive task in combination with a content knowledge task. For each question that students answer, they also indicate one of the following four choices:

> I knew it.
> I figured it out.
> I guessed at it.
> I don't care.

During one discussion, the group started with a question that troubled a number of students (see Figure 7.4). Mr. Jacobs said, "Let's start with question 3. Only 61 percent of the students got it right, and only 38 percent of them self-reported that they knew it. According to the same self-assessment, an additional 36 percent had 'figured it out,' and 24 percent indicated that they 'guessed at it.' It's interesting that only 3 kids (of 241) didn't care about this question. I know that I taught this, but most of the wrong answers were still based on democracy, just not the right type of democracy. I think this could be a quick fix. We need to make sure that students really have a sense of the difference between direct and representative democracy. I have an idea for a simulation that could really solidify this concept for students." Mr. Jacobs proceeded to describe his idea for a simulation, and the teachers agreed to reteach this concept.

Figure 7.4
Sample History Questions and Results

3. In a(n) _____, all citizens at mass meetings make decisions for the government.
   A. monarchy
   B. oligarchy
   C. direct democracy
   D. representative democracy

3. Student answer percentages:
   A. 7%
   B. 2%
   C. 61% (correct answer)
   D. 30%

10. Use the map below to answer the following question: Sparta is located _____ of Athens.
   A. northwest
   B. northeast
   C. southwest
   D. southeast

10. Student answer percentages:
   A. 10%
   B. 3%
   C. 58% (correct answer)
   D. 29%

From the students' self-assessment, the teachers determined a correlation between correctness and a confident response in "knowing" the answer. Also, accuracy was evident in the "figuring it out" indicator. The teachers were pleased to see that their students were using the test-taking strategies of elimination and context clues.

Mrs. Johnson then turned their attention to question 10 and said, "Here we go again. Our students still don't have a sense of the cardinal points. We keep asking them questions that require them to use map skills, but they are getting them wrong. Look here, just over 50 percent correct. We have to focus on interpreting maps every day. It's not just about using this for history and geography. This is a life skill."

Ms. Vasquez confessed, "I don't really know how to teach this. I've shown my students the map and the directions. I don't know what to do differently so that they learn this." Mrs. Johnson suggested that Ms. Vasquez visit another teacher's class and observe, offering, "I'll cover your class so that you can go observe Mr. Applegate. Is that okay? Then we can talk further about reteaching the concept of cardinal points. Does anyone else need help with this? Only half of our students are getting this!" Mrs. Johnson also suggested that the group consider revising the pacing guide to allow more time to teach map skills.

The group continued to analyze the results and in the process identified a small group of students who would benefit from additional instruction to build background knowledge. These students were found to have missed all of the items related to government structures, and the group suspected that they lacked background knowledge in this area. To address these concerns, Mr. Applegate met with these students during the after-school program.

Identifying Competencies for Course Mastery

While common formative assessments like those mentioned serve as valuable benchmarks for informing instruction, they offer only snapshots of student progress. Learners also need a system to help them measure their attainment of course goals. The educational literature is rich with advice on the importance of establishing goals to motivate student learning (Wigfield & Eccles, 2002). These goals need to be a balance of short-term objectives ("I'm going to ask good questions today") and long-term objectives ("I'm going to pass biology"). However, the gap that exists between these goals can be overwhelming. The use of a competency system for establishing concrete course performance objectives allows students to measure their progress throughout a course (*feed-up*). Course competencies are designed by grade-level teachers or department administrators and are intended to capture the state standards while providing students with an array of ways to demonstrate mastery. The grades earned on these competencies determine the student's grade for the course, but teachers reserve the right to add or subtract up to 10 percent based on attitude, behavior, and participation in classroom tasks (*feedback*).

It is important not to rely solely on paper-and-pencil tasks, as it short-changes students and disregards the breadth of the content standards. The number of competencies also needs to be sufficient—usually 7 to 10 per year—so that students are able to adequately gauge their progress. Competencies for 5th grade social studies might include an oral presentation on the cultures of various American Indian tribes, a map illustrating explorers' routes, a traditional multiple-choice and short-answer test on cooperation and conflict between American Indian tribes and settlers, and a readers' theater script written and performed on the early history of the American colonies.

Competencies for 9th and 10th grade English might include four essays based on each term's schoolwide essential questions, two literature response essays (given in the fall and in the spring), an oral language competency that includes retelling and a dramatic monologue, a poetry portfolio, and tests on persuasive techniques and summarizing. For example, formal essays are an important part of one high school's course, so the teachers explain that the two-week unit on plagiarizing will help them with this task (*feed-up*). The teachers have already developed a common formative assessment so that they can discuss results and analyze patterns (*feedback*). Students are required to cite works from a variety of documents, including a newspaper article, a Web site, a book with two or more authors, and an interview. The results indicate that many students still are not able to correctly cite Web site resources. Knowing that this will be a crucial part of their first competency essay, the teachers reteach the specifics of this type of citation and use students' incorrect answers for error analysis (*feed-forward*).

State Assessments

A nested system of assessments should build toward state tests that measure the progress of students and schools. While we do not believe that cramming a few weeks full of "test-prep" worksheets is particularly useful, we do believe that students should understand that tests are a genre—one that they are capable of mastering. We advocate the ongoing use of assessments throughout the year that collectively build toward "test wiseness" so that students have regular exposure to test format within their everyday instruction. For example, a math teacher thinks aloud while completing a multiple-choice problem that requires adding fractions (1/7 + 3/7). She eliminates distractors by saying, "I see one of the choices has 14 as a denominator, but I know we don't add the denominators when adding fractions, so that can't be a correct choice." Similarly, as part of their competency on persuasive writing techniques, 10th grade English students learn methods to begin a compelling essay by focusing on writing introductions to topics they didn't choose. This is performed in anticipation of their high school exit exam, which includes on-demand writing. By embedding format practice within daily checking-for-understanding tasks, common formative assessments, and course competency exams, students acquire both the stamina and the skills they will need to be successful on state accountability assessments.

What the Ancient Mariner Can Teach Us

Samuel Taylor Coleridge's epic poem *The Rime of the Ancient Mariner* is a cautionary tale about failing to learn from one's mistakes. The mariner was doomed to walk the earth telling strangers of his error in killing an albatross that had saved his ship's crew from disaster. It is easy to view the sea of assessment data around us as a liability simply because we don't know what to do with it all. By viewing the assessment process as a nested system that provides the power to feed-up, feedback, and feed-forward, we can avoid mistaking help for hindrance. As with our students, it's never too late to learn this important lesson.

The Takeaway

After you have read this chapter, consider these key points:

• Feed-up processes allow students to understand the goal of instruction, which in turn makes them more likely to focus on the learning tasks at hand.

• Feedback must be considered as a system, not simply information provided to individual students based on their performance.

• Feed-forward systems in which student work is used to plan instruction and intervention is critical to the implementation of RTI[2].

• Progress monitoring requires an alignment of checking for understanding with other assessments, including course competencies and summative tools.

8

Leading RTI^2 Efforts:
Hardwiring Excellence

Thus far, we have discussed the various components of a systematic Response to Instruction and Intervention effort. All of these components are critical if schools wish to become high achieving, but the components must become ingrained in the operating system of each and every classroom, and of the school in general. For RTI^2 to work, it has to become accepted and institutionalized, not a special program that individual teachers can opt into or out of. It has to be hardwired into the very culture of the school.

The concept of hardwiring excellence comes from the healthcare industry. Quint Studer (2003) suggested that individuals want to be part of organizations when they agree with the organization's purpose, they believe that their work is worthwhile, and they feel that they can make a difference. Although Studer was writing about hospitals, these three conditions also fit nicely with our experiences as teachers. Purpose, worthwhile work, and making a difference are certainly motivators for the teachers and administrators we know. However, Studer took it further, saying that the organization needs a system for recognizing what's successful and what's not working well. When that system is put into place, excellence becomes hardwired into the organization. For educators, that system is RTI^2.

In a shocking and sobering quote, Studer also notes, "The fish starts rotting at the head" (p. 12) and recommends that organizational change directed at hardwiring excellence begins with the leadership. Evidence for the importance of effective leadership in schools is compelling. According to Waters, Marzano, and McNulty (2003), the average effect size between leadership and student achievement is 0.25. Effect size is a statistical tool that measures the relationship between two variables. They explain this correlation as follows:

> Consider two schools (school A & school B) with similar student and teacher populations. Both demonstrate achievement on a standardized, norm-referenced test at the 50th percentile. Principals in both schools are also average—that is, their abilities in the 21 key leadership responsibilities are ranked at the 50th percentile. Now assume that the principal of school B improves her demonstrated abilities in all 21 responsibilities by exactly one standard deviation.... Our research findings indicate that this increase in leadership ability would translate into mean student achievement at school B that is 10 percentile points higher than school A. (p. 3)

What's a Leader to Do?

After many years of working inside and outside schools, we've come to realize that the single most important thing that a school leader can do is reach agreement with the staff about quality. Quality is the driving force behind hardwiring excellence, and it's what nearly every employee strives for. There is no doubt that the vast majority of teachers wakes up every morning and goes to work to do the very best job possible.

Therein, as they say, lies the rub. There is not a universally accepted definition of "the best job" or general agreement about quality indicators. This is as evident in the analysis of student work as it is in teacher behavior. Consider this scenario:

> David hasn't done much of his algebra homework. He's missed school a lot but has been excused by his grandmother for every absence. Going into the final exam, he has an *F* in the class (34 percent), but he's been working with a tutor and gets an *A* on the cumulative final exam, which is worth 15 percent of the total class grade. What grade should he get in the class?

Of course, there is no "right" answer to this question. When we asked an audience of more than 100 teachers to write down the grade that they would give David, the responses included the full range of grades from *A* to *F*. Every teacher there had a perfectly reasonable rationale for the grade he or she assigned. David's specific grade isn't the issue here; rather, it's the lack of agreement about the meaning of quality. In this case, does quality mean demonstrating understanding of the standards, doing homework, attending class, or some combination of them all?

A similar phenomenon happens when groups of teachers look at student work, which is why Langer, Colton, and Goff (2003) developed an entire protocol to help teachers analyze student work. Of course, part of an effective RTI[2] effort requires that teachers independently recognize high-quality student work and have assessment systems for collecting and analyzing this work.

The same thing also occurs when teachers observe one another in the classroom. Without an agreement on quality, peer observations, coaching, and administrative feedback are ineffective. In fact, we would argue that teachers are immune to feedback from a coach or administrator when they have different definitions of quality. We've observed situations like this over and over again. Following a classroom observation, the teacher asks, "How do you think it went?" The observer responds, "How do *you* think it went?" The conversation then continues:

> *Teacher:* Pretty well. They all seemed to like it.
>
> *Observer:* Yes, that's true. During your modeling, did you consider making your thinking process clear?
>
> *Teacher:* My thinking was pretty clear. They knew what to do after the modeling. But yeah, I could probably get better at that.
>
> *Observer:* I was wondering about modeling and how it helps English language learners. You might want to think about that and try some metacognitive modeling.
>
> *Teacher:* Yeah, I should. I think I do that a lot. Today was a bit different because we were reviewing.
>
> *Observer:* Oh. Were the students pretty familiar with the content already?
>
> *Teacher:* Yes. They've been working on this, and I wanted to do a bit of a review for them.

This conversation continues for several more minutes, with neither participant changed as a result of the interaction.

The conversation is vastly different when both parties have a clear understanding of quality. In some cases, quality can be defined by creating rubrics as a group so that the words represent ideas that both the observer and the teacher understand. The classroom observation rubric in Figure 8.1 is an example that we developed as part of the San Diego Peer Coaching

Figure 8.1
Classroom Observation Rubric

Reviewer: _____   Candidate: _____

Indicate how well the candidate demonstrated the expectations shown below (maximum points = 20).

Expectations	Evaluator's Notes	1 Inadequate	2	3	4 Expert	Total
		(Little or no evidence)			*(Consistently apparent; featured throughout for all students)*	
Engaging and supporting students in learning as evidenced by the following: • Teacher builds on students' prior knowledge. • Teacher uses a variety of instructional routines designed to engage and motivate students. • Teacher responds to students in a supportive way. • Teacher provides positive and constructive feedback on student learning. • Students are engaged in learning activities.						
Establishing high expectations for students as evidenced by the following: • Teacher actively engages students in problem solving and critical thinking. • Teacher assists students to become self-directed learners who are able to demonstrate, articulate, and evaluate what they learn. • Students are encouraged to raise questions. • Teacher encourages students to construct explanations for their ideas and responses. • Teacher presents lessons that are challenging yet engaging.						

Assessing student learning as evidenced by the following:

- Teacher establishes and clearly communicates learning goal for students.
- Teacher collects information about student performance from a variety of sources.
- Teacher uses information from a variety of ongoing assessments to plan and adjust learning opportunities.
- Teacher provides the criteria for assessing student work.

Creating and maintaining effective environments for student learning as evidenced by the following:

- Teacher creates a print-rich environment.
- Teacher creates a learning environment as a tool for learning.
- The physical environment is arranged to engage students in purposeful learning activities and encourage constructive interactions among students.
- Teacher maintains an environment in which students are treated fairly and respectfully.

Understanding and organizing literacy instruction as evidenced by the following:

- Teacher implements grouping format(s) appropriate to the lesson.
- Teacher's instruction reflects interactions between and among the language arts (reading, writing, speaking, and listening).
- Instruction reflects a firm understanding of theory and research in language development and second language acquisition.

Grand Total =

Project in partnership with Nancy Farnan, Leif Fearn, Diane Lapp, and James Flood. When both the observer and the teacher have a shared definition of quality, the interaction is more worthwhile. Here's an excerpt of such a conversation:

> *Teacher:* I think my students were very engaged in this lesson, but I'm not sure that they felt comfortable enough to ask questions.
>
> *Observer:* I noticed the same thing. I'm not sure if it's because of the content or the instructional routine you used, but I did notice the lack of questions from students.
>
> *Teacher:* Did I encourage them enough? Could I have done that better?
>
> *Observer:* I really appreciated the way you paused to model questioning, so I didn't get the sense that that was the issue. You were very encouraging. I wonder if they needed more time in their productive group work.
>
> *Teacher:* Good point. That would have given me more time to collect some assessment information.
>
> *Observer:* I hadn't thought about that. Yes, more assessment information might have helped you think about what you needed to do to facilitate inquiry. What assessments did you have time to collect?

This conversation continues for several more minutes, with each participant referring to items on the rubric and their shared understanding of what it means to provide quality instruction.

Of course, there are a number of duties assigned to the school leader; instructional leadership is just one of them. However, instructional leadership means more than simply telling people what to do. It means leading people through a process of improvement, much like the action research work advocated by Calhoun (1994). As we noted in Chapter 7, this process requires the use of feedback. Just as it does with students, teacher feedback needs to involve all three components: feed-up, feedback, and feed-forward. As we have articulated, this feedback is effective only when the person receiving it and the person providing it are in agreement about quality. When the leader accomplishes this and has created an understanding of quality, his or her job is suddenly much easier.

The Role of the Family in RTI²

The family is also essential to the RTI² process, because family members are the ones who, as our colleague Barbara Buswell consistently reminds us, "are the keepers of the child's history." We like to think of them as the home-based administrators. Families are not an afterthought in RTI^2, merely there so we can check off a box that indicates parent involvement. Indeed, they provide valuable information about what has worked in the past as well as what has been unsuccessful. Families also provide motivation, praise, and encouragement that can ensure success.

It's important that we don't construct school-based processes that make it difficult for families to participate. Many schools have already undertaken family involvement and empowerment initiatives, and RTI^2 information should be integrated into those supports. Some schools have parent centers that offer translation and advocacy supports to families, and these providers should be equipped with the technical information needed. For some families, attending meetings during school hours may be difficult; creative communication measures might include hosting Web-based conversations or making home or community visits.

Family involvement also occurs between meetings. Intervention assessments can be great communication tools. For example, in Chapter 6, 5th grade teacher Mr. Robertson kept in touch with Christopher's family by sending a report home each week. He was collecting data to monitor his student's progress, but this information was also a valuable update for Christopher's family. Using a simple template designed by his school's RTI^2 committee, Mr. Robertson was able to send a note home every Friday (see Figure 8.2).

The Role of the Coach in RTI^2

The value of coaching has only increased with the widespread institution of Response to Instruction and Intervention efforts. Now, more than ever, every school needs people who are skilled at brokering conversations, demonstrating instructional approaches, and providing technical assistance in collecting and analyzing data. Coaches come under many names, including reading and math specialists, resource teachers, and peer coaches. Whatever the title, this position can serve as the linchpin for coordinating RTI^2 efforts throughout a school.

The effectiveness of coaching has been studied widely during recent years, and it has been shown to be a highly beneficial practice for teachers. One of the most compelling arguments for their involvement is that coaching empowers teachers as change agents by integrating innovative practices with collegial interactions (Weasmer & Woods, 1999). Indeed,

Figure 8.2
Family Report on Student Progress

Wilson Elementary School
Progress Report

Date: ___4/3/2011___

To the parent/guardian of: _____Christopher_____

From: _____Dan Robertson_____

Your child has been working toward a goal of _____building fluency with multiplication facts_____.

I wanted to share this report of progress on his/her work in this area.

Chris did a great job this week. He is showing gains on the one-minute timed test for math facts up to 12x12. His score today was 32/50, a gain over last week's score of 30/50.

Your encouragement means a lot to Chris and definitely helps him with his learning. Thanks for your continued support.

Sincerely,

Mr. Robertson

---

problem solving necessitates a collaborative approach that allows for continuous improvement in instruction. The active work of coaches improves achievement as well. A study by Mallette, Maheady, and Harper (1999) suggests that coaching is particularly effective in supporting the achievement of students with diverse learning needs, many of whom find themselves receiving instruction and intervention supports.

Effective coaching requires that the coach perform his or her role in ways that encourage growth in others. Characteristics include knowledge of the subject matter, written and oral communication skills, the ability to teach through demonstration, and the ability to detect and avoid creating obstacles to learning (Mager, 1999). The inability to perform these complex tasks, a common phenomenon with inexperienced coaches, can undermine the overall coaching effort (Perkins, 1998). For this reason, it is important to identify candidates who possess the qualities necessary for this work. Excellence in the classroom is essential, of course, but it is not the only requirement. A coach must also be able to work collaboratively with administrators, fellow teachers, and families. We recommend following Burkins's (2009) advice to interview coaching candidates with questions such as

• How do your experiences, training, and education prepare you for the duties and responsibilities of coaching?

• If you were asked to lead a professional development workshop on an aspect of RTI^2, what topic would you choose to discuss? What would you include in your workshop?

• In your opinion, how do content standards and best practices for RTI^2 inform one another?

• What misconceptions about teachers need to be dispelled? About families? About administrators? About struggling learners?

• What do you think teachers will expect of you as a coach, and how will you meet those expectations?

• What excites you about coaching? What concerns do you have about coaching?

The Role of the Teacher in RTI^2

We regard the focus on teacher collaboration as a major achievement in Response to Instruction and Intervention. As one teacher remarked, "Finally! All these years we've said we needed to stop focusing on job descriptions and focus instead on students. I don't have to sneak around anymore just to talk to a colleague."

You may have noticed that we addressed this section to teachers. Not *special education* teachers, *algebra* teachers, or *classroom* teachers. Just teachers. As educators who have worn multiple hats over the years, we have come to appreciate the way these knowledge bases merge. While we have areas of specialization that allow us to contribute unique perspectives, the fundamentals of our trade are common: we teach for meaningful learning using instructional approaches that are responsive to the intellectual, academic, psychological, and emotional needs of our students. As special educators, we were frustrated that our knowledge could not benefit children without IEPs. As general educators, we found it inconceivable that we were pigeonholed into a grade level or departmental slot, with little contact with other teachers in the same building. As reading and language specialists, we witnessed how much time and effort was wasted on creating individualized interventions that bore little relationship to the core curriculum. The RTI^2 process allows us to engage in a practice that is generally regarded as common sense—consulting with others to build professional knowledge.

The power of these collaborative efforts extends to the systems level. The collective wisdom of educators and families exceeds anything that could be contained within a book or manual, particularly because every organization possesses inherent strengths. Teachers possess much (but not all) of this strength, but they don't often get to share it because there is no dedicated forum in which to do so. RTI^2 is the game-changer we've been waiting for.

The National Education Association identified several roles that teachers should play during system design, including

• Identifying and analyzing existing literature on problem solving and RTI in order to determine a relevant and effective approach for the local district.

• Actively identifying and addressing systemic barriers to learning.

• Identifying, implementing, documenting, and analyzing evidence-based academic interventions.

• Identifying, implementing, documenting, and analyzing evidence-based behavioral interventions.

• Identifying technology needs and reviewing technology programs to reduce increased paperwork expectations.

• Engaging in ongoing communication and consultation with administrators, school board members, related service providers, and parents.

• Identifying professional development topics and issues of importance to the process. (2006, p. 42)

Of course, classroom teachers also play a key role in the actual implementation of RTI^2 efforts, including classroom instruction, data collection and analysis, and participation on committees that coordinate schoolwide efforts. We've focused on each of these roles in other parts of this book; now we turn our attention to the work of the committee.

The Role of the RTI^2 Committee

While not all committees are useful, the RTI^2 committee can be invaluable for improving schooling for students, their families, and the educators who work with them. As we have reported numerous times throughout this book, the RTI^2 committee's charge is to oversee the efforts of the school in order to foster effective instruction and intervention for students, use data to analyze school instruction and intervention, and promote coordination and communication among stakeholders. It is important to make sure that the committee is not overburdened with tasks so that they can focus on this work. For example, the RTI^2 committee should not supplant the mission of the Student Study Team, whose job it is to make recommendations about referrals for special education testing. (Keep in mind that there are other students at the school for whom difficulties other than identified learning disabilities are suspected.)

Coordination

Scheduling intervention supports can be complex in a busy school. The committee can advise on scheduling practices with an eye toward creating time for educators to collaborate. In addition, standing agenda items for data examination and analysis must be included. At our school, an item called "Spotlight" is on every agenda; this time is devoted to discussing the progress of students who are showing early signs of falling behind but who are not yet receiving formal Tier 2 supports. Another standing agenda item at the monthly meetings is devoted to linking the lessons learned at the grade and department levels to classroom practice. For example, the decision by the 5th grade team in Chapter 6 to include math facts as part of their daily warm-up grew out of a conversation in the RTI^2 committee about the number of students who were benefiting from this kind of practice.

Communication

The RTI^2 committee should also make recommendations about ways to increase communication among stakeholders. One school's committee suggested a standing e-mail reminder—for teachers who had students participating in interventions—to send home updates to families. These weekly e-mails served as an excellent reminder for busy teachers. A committee at a school where families speak 17 different languages invited the parent services coordinator to advise them on ways to make communication more family-friendly. One outcome of this meeting was the development of simple report templates translated into multiple languages that allowed teachers to supply data to families in their native languages.

Collaboration

The composition of the RTI[2] committee should reflect the stakeholders mentioned previously in this chapter. Family representation is vital, especially in advising the committee about innovative ways to promote communication. In addition, teacher representation by grade level or department is essential. Representatives can advise the committee about curriculum and instruction and bring questions and recommendations back to their respective teams. Administrative leadership is also important, as few things are more frustrating than formulating ideas or questions with no outlet for follow-up. Finally, the coach is a critical team member because he or she facilitates so much of the day-to-day collaboration necessary for RTI[2] to work.

The Takeaway

As with all of the other chapters, we end this chapter with key ideas and concepts we hope are useful in improving schools:

• Site leaders are critical to the implementation of RTI[2].

• High-performing systems have agreed-upon definitions of quality. These agreements extend to discussions of quality student work and quality instruction and intervention.

• Every member of the school community, including parents, teachers, coaches, and the RTI[2] committee, has a role to play in the implementation of RTI[2].

Choose Your Adventure:
Where RTI^2 Can Take Our Students

You first met Adam in Chapter 1, when he was a 5th grade student at a new school. Fortunately, he attended a school where instruction and intervention were central to the school's mission of educating students. When we left Adam, he was entering 6th grade as a confident student—still in need of support but not in danger of getting lost. Fast-forward a few years, and Adam is getting ready to graduate from high school. While some of his academic courses posed a challenge at times, his middle and high schools were poised to support struggling learners.

Freshman year of high school is difficult for many students because of the many social and academic demands, and Adam's was no exception. Soon after Adam entered 9th grade, he fell behind. Fortunately, the school's academic recovery efforts were in place, and, before the first quarter was over, he received homework support once a week. "Adam has been a 'frequent flyer' around here," remarked Mr. Houston, the coordinator. "The thing is, we get kids like him on our radar pretty early so we can be proactive." Adam's guidance counselor, Ms. Jacoby, also played a role. "There were a few times when I did some hand-scheduling for Adam," she explained. "English is always hard for him, so I met with the English department chair, and she made recommendations for his classes. In fact, [the department chair] taught him in 10th grade because she said she believed she was the most qualified to give him the extra support he sometimes needed."

Adam's parents have remained involved, even though they found it more difficult as Adam got older. "He's a typical teenager," said his mother, "but the school has made it easy for us. His grades are posted online so we can view them 24/7, even though Adam acts like he doesn't like it." His parents also praised his teachers. "They were great about responding to e-mails," Adam's dad said. "When we had a question, we felt like we could ask it without being too much of a pain."

Adam is now looking forward to classes at community college. "I'm going to stay local and get my AA [associate's degree], then transfer to the university," he said. "I know I need a bit of a safety net, so I want to take small steps. I've had some great teachers and great schools since I moved to this town." In what is perhaps the highest compliment of all, Adam tells us he plans on becoming a physical education teacher "so I can help kids, too."

Throughout this book, we've provided details about the implementation of an effective Response to Instruction and Intervention effort. When instruction and intervention are aligned, and assessments drive instruction, students learn. It really is that simple. With this in mind, we'd like to close with a few points that deserve repeated attention.

We have to hold high expectations for students and ourselves. We must have systems of support to ensure that students can reach these high expectations, but we start with high expectations. This means, in part, that teachers must teach the appropriate grade-level standards. An excellent, highly engaging, interactive lesson that is based on below-level standards will not ensure that students reach high levels of achievement. While this point may seem obvious, we've seen too many well-meaning teachers who, for whatever reason, are teaching below grade-level expectations. As we were writing this book, we observed a 4th grade lesson that was fantastic. The problem was that it focused on 2nd grade standards. This resulted in a group of students who performed well below grade level, despite good instruction.

We have to focus on high-quality core instruction, first and foremost. As we have noted, supplemental and intensive interventions cannot compensate for poor core instruction. If the vast majority of students—70 percent or so—are not meeting grade-level expectations or demonstrating a full year's growth for each year of schooling, the core program must be reexamined. The answer to this problem does not lie in supplemental intervention programs, despite the promise they hold, but rather in the engagement of professional development, coaching, feedback, and a core program review.

We have to make sure that instruction and intervention are linked. Supplemental and intensive interventions should build on the students' experiences with the core program and facilitate student achievement of the standards expected for their grade level. Unfortunately, there are far too many supplemental programs for sale that take students away from the core program. Often, the result is that students experience failure in two arenas: the core curriculum *and* the supplemental curriculum.

We have to manipulate a number of variables (time, assessment, expertise, and instruction) to intensify intervention. RTI^2 is not simply about requiring students to attend more school (although in some cases that is exactly what is needed). As teachers and administrators, we have to remember that there are a number of variables that we can manipulate to ensure that students succeed. As we discussed early in this book, instruction and time used to be held constant while achievement was allowed to vary. Today, we know better—we vary instruction and time in order to hold achievement constant.

We have to build in a feed-forward method so that RTI^2 results inform classroom instruction and programmatic improvements. In other words, assessment is critical in an RTI^2 effort. It's not enough to simply collect assessment information, formative or summative. It's what we do with the assessment information that matters. In highly successful educational systems, assessments drive instruction. Of course, this statement assumes that the assessments are linked to standards and grade-level expectations. It also assumes that assessment information can be accessed quickly and easily so that teachers can plan instruction and intervention.

We have to keep the teacher and family at the center of communication. We are reminded of colleagues who said, "We are temporary members of the student's life; the parents are there for the long haul" and "The parents send us the best kid they've got; they don't keep the good ones at home." Together, students, families, teachers, support personnel, and administrators can change the lives of every child. Someday, a child like Adam will grow up and send you a note of thanks, like the one we received:

> I just want to thank you for all the things you have done for me. You helped me grow into a better man in school and at home. I never thought school could be like this. I look forward to school next year, and I never did look forward to school before. Someday I will be going to college and could pay it forward, like you said.
>
> Adam

References

Achebe, C. (2008). *Things fall apart*. New York: Norton.

Alexander, K. L., Entwisle, D. R., & Olson, L. S. (2007). Lasting consequences of the summer learning gap. *American Sociological Review, 72,* 167–180.

Allington, R. L. (2001). *What really matters for struggling readers: Designing research-based programs*. New York: Longman.

Allington, R. L. (2009). *What really matters in response to intervention: Research-based designs*. Boston: Allyn and Bacon.

Alvermann, D. E., & Rush, L. S. (2004). Literacy intervention programs at the middle and high school levels. In T. L. Jetton & J. A. Dole (Eds.), *Adolescent literacy research and practice* (pp. 210–227). New York: The Guilford Press.

Ashton-Warner, S. (1959). *Spinster*. New York: Simon & Schuster.

Baker, S., Gersten, R., & Lee, D. S. (2002). A synthesis of empirical research on teaching mathematics to low-achieving students. *Elementary School Journal, 103*(1), 51–73.

Barnett, D. W., Daly, E. J., III, Jones, K. M., & Lentz, F. E., Jr. (2004). Response to intervention: Empirically based special service decisions from single-case designs of increasing and decreasing intensity. *The Journal of Special Education, 38*(2), 66–79.

Beavers, J. (1999). *Developmental reading assessment*. Parsippany, NJ: Celebration.

Beckman, M. (1990). Collaborative learning: Preparation for the workplace and democracy. *College Teaching, 38*(4), 128–133.

Bolt, S. E., & Thurlow, M. L. (2004). Five of the most commonly allowed accommodations in state policy: Synthesis of research. *Remedial and Special Education, 25,* 141–152.

Brookhart, S. M. (2008). *How to give effective feedback to your students*. Alexandria, VA: ASCD.

Bryant, D. P., Bryant, B. R., Gersten, G. M., Scammacca, N. N., Funk, C., Winter, A., Shih, M., & Pool, C. (2008). The effects of Tier 2 intervention on the mathematics performance of first-grade students who are at risk for mathematics difficulty. *Learning Disability Quarterly, 31*(2), 47–63.

Buffum, A., Mattos, M., & Weber, C. (2009). *Pyramid response to intervention: RTI, professional learning communities, and how to respond when kids don't learn*. Bloomington, IN: Solution Tree.

Burkins, J. (2009). *Practical literacy coaching: A collection of tools to support your work*. Newark, DE: International Reading Association.

Calhoun, E. F. (1994). *How to use action research in the self-renewing school*. Alexandria, VA: ASCD.

California Department of Education. (2009). Resources—RtI². Retrieved July 6, 2009, from www.cde.ca.gov/ci/cr/ri/rtiresources.asp

Cobb, C. (2007). Training paraprofessionals to work effectively with all students. *The Reading Teacher, 60*(7), 686–689.

Cole, S., Horvath, B., Chapman, C., Deschenes, C., Ebeling, D., & Sprague, J. (2000). *Adapting curriculum and instruction in inclusive classrooms: A teacher's desk reference* (2nd ed.). Bloomington, IN: Indiana Institute on Disability and Community.

Colon, J. (1982). *A Puerto Rican in New York, and other sketches* (2nd ed.). New York: International Publishers.

Deno, S. (2003). Developments in curriculum-based measurements. *Journal of Special Education, 37*(3), 184–192.

Desimone, L. (2002). How can comprehensive school reform models be successfully implemented? *Review of Educational Research, 72,* 433–480.

Diamond, M., & Hopson, J. (1998). *Magic trees of the mind: How to nurture your child's intelligence, creativity and healthy emotions from birth through adolescence.* New York: Dutton.

Dixon, C., & Nessel, D. (1983). *Language experience approach to reading (and writing): Language experience reading for second language learners.* Hayward, CA: Alemany.

Dong, Y. R. (2004/2005). Getting at the content. *Educational Leadership, 62,* 14–19.

Duffy, G. G. (2003). *Explaining reading: A resource for teaching concepts, skills, and strategies.* New York: The Guilford Press.

Dutro, S., & Moran, C. (2003). Rethinking English language instruction: An architectural approach. In G. G. Garcia (Ed.), *English learners: Reaching the highest level of English literacy* (pp. 227–258). Newark, DE: International Reading Association.

Elbaum, B., Vaughn, S., Hughes, M. T., & Moody, S. (2000). How effective are one-to-one tutoring programs in reading for elementary students at risk for reading failure? A meta-analysis of the intervention research. *Journal of Educational Psychology, 92,* 605–619.

Espin, C., Wallace, T., Lembke, E. S., Long, J. D., & Ticha, R. (2008). Curriculum-based measurement in writing: Predicting the success of high-school students on state standards tests. *Exceptional Children, 74*(2), 174–193.

Fisher, D. (2001). "We're moving on up": Creating a schoolwide literacy effort in an urban high school. *Journal of Adolescent & Adult Literacy, 45,* 92–101.

Fisher, D. (2004). Setting the "opportunity to read" standard: Resuscitating the SSR program in an urban high school. *Journal of Adolescent & Adult Literacy, 48,* 138–150.

Fisher, D., & Frey, N. (2007a). *Checking for understanding: Formative assessment techniques for your classroom.* Alexandria, VA: ASCD.

Fisher, D., & Frey, N. (2007b). *Scaffolded writing instruction: Teaching with a gradual-release framework.* New York: Scholastic.

Fisher, D., & Frey, N. (2008). *Better learning through structured teaching: A framework for the gradual release of responsibility.* Alexandria, VA: ASCD.

Fisher, D., & Frey, N. (2009). *Building background knowledge.* Portsmouth, NH: Heinemann.

Fisher, D., Frey, N., & Lapp, D. (2008). Shared readings: Modeling comprehension, vocabulary, text structures, and text features for older readers. *The Reading Teacher, 61,* 548–557.

Fisher, D., Frey, N., & Lapp, D. (2009). Meeting AYP in a high need school: A formative experiment. *Journal of Adolescent & Adult Literacy, 52,* 386–396.

Fisher, D., Grant, M., Frey, N., & Johnson, C. (2007). Taking formative assessments schoolwide. *Educational Leadership, 65*(4), 64–68.

Fisher, D., & Ivey, G. (2006). Evaluating the interventions for struggling adolescent readers. *Journal of Adolescent & Adult Literacy, 50,* 180–189.

Foorman, B., & Torgesen, J. (2001). Critical elements of classroom and small-group instruction promote reading success in all children. *Learning Disabilities Research and Practice, 16,* 203–212.

Frey, N. (2003). The gift of time: Providing literacy support to first grade struggling readers in an urban Professional Development School. *Dissertation Abstracts International, 64*(2), 402.

Frey, N. (2006). The role of 1:1 individual instruction in reading. *Theory into Practice, 45*(3), 207–214.

Frey, N. (2007). *Partnerships in RtI: A tale of two triangles.* Keynote presentation at the 2007 Conference on Inclusive Education, Denver, CO.

Frey, N., & Fisher, D. (2009). *Learning words inside and out: Vocabulary instruction that boosts achievement in all subject areas.* Portsmouth, NH: Heinemann.

Frey, N., Fisher, D., & Everlove, S. (2009). *Productive group work: How to engage students, build teamwork, and promote understanding.* Alexandria, VA: ASCD.

Frey, N., Fisher, D., & Moore, K. (2009). Literacy letters: Comparative literature and formative assessment. *The ALAN Review, 36*(2), 27–33.

Gersten, R., Beckman, S., Clarke, B., Foegen, A., Marsh, L., Star, J. R., & Witzel, B. (2009). *Assisting students struggling with mathematics: Response to intervention (RtI) for elementary and middle schools* (NCEE 2009-4060). Washington, DC: National Center for Education Evaluation and Regional Assistance, Institute for Education Sciences, U.S. Department of Education. Retrieved July 7, 2009, from http://ies.ed.gov/ncee/wwc/publications/practiceguides

Gersten, R., Compton, D., Connor, C. M., Dimino, J., Santoro, L., Linan-Thompson, S., & Tilly, W. D. (2009). *Assisting students struggling with reading: Response to intervention (RtI) and multi-tier intervention in the primary grades* (NCEE 2009-4045). Washington, DC: National Center for Education Evaluation and Regional Assistance, Institute for Education Sciences, U.S. Department of Education. Retrieved July 7, 2009, from http://ies.ed.gov/ncee/wwc/publications/practiceguides

Gersten, R., & Dimino, J. A. (2006). RTI (Response to Intervention): Rethinking special education for students with reading difficulties (yet again). *Reading Research Quarterly, 41*(1), 99–108.

Good, R. H., Gruba, J., & Kaminski, R. (2002). Best practice in using Dynamic Indicators of Basic Early Literacy Skills (DIBELS) in an outcomes-driven model. In A. Thomas & Grimes (Eds.), *Best practices in school psychology IV* (pp. 699–720). Bethesda, MD: NASP Publications.

Goodman, Y. (1985). Kidwatching: Observing children in the classroom. In A. Jaggar & M. T. Smith-Burke (Eds.), *Observing the language learner* (pp. 9–18). Newark, DE: International Reading Association.

Guthrie, J. T. (1996). Educational contexts for engagement in literacy. *The Reading Teacher, 49,* 432–445.

Hasbrouck, J., & Tindal, G. A. (2006). Oral fluency norms. A valuable assessment tool for reading teachers. *The Reading Teacher, 59*(7), 636–644.

Hattie, J., & Timperley, H. (2007). The power of feedback. *Review of Educational Research, 77,* 81–112.

Heritage, M. (2009). Using self-assessment to chart students' paths. *Middle School Journal, 40*(5), 27–30.

Hill, J. D., & Flynn, K. M. (2006). *Classroom instruction that works with English language learners.* Alexandria, VA: ASCD.

Hinton, S. E. (2006). *The outsiders.* New York: Puffin.

Hosp, J. L. (2006). Assessment practices and response to intervention. *NASP Communiqué, 34*(7). Retrieved July 15, 2009, from www.nasponline.org/publications/cq/cq347rti.aspx

Ivey, G. (1999). A multicase study in the middle school: Complexities among young adolescent readers. *Reading Research Quarterly, 34,* 172–192.

Ivey, G. (2004). Content counts with urban struggling readers. In D. Lapp, C. C. Block, E. J. Cooper, J. Flood, N. Roser, & J. V. Tinajero (Eds.), *Teaching all the children: Strategies for developing literacy in an urban setting* (pp. 316–326). New York: The Guilford Press.

Ivey, G., & Broaddus, K. (2001). "Just plain reading": A survey of what makes students want to read in middle school classrooms. *Reading Research Quarterly, 36*(4), 350–371.

Ivey, G., & Fisher, D. (2006). When thinking skills trump reading skills. *Educational Leadership, 64*(2), 16–21.

Jimenez, F. (1999). *The circuit.* New York: Houghton Mifflin.

Johnston, P. H. (1987). Teachers as evaluation experts. *The Reading Teacher, 40,* 744–748.

Johnston, P. H., & Allington, R. L. (1991). Remediation. In R. Barr, M. L. Kamil, P. Mosenthal, & P. D. Pearson (Eds.), *Handbook of reading research* (Vol. 2, pp. 984–1012). New York: Longman.

Johnston, P. H., & Winograd, P. N. (1985). Passive failure in reading. *Journal of Reading Behavior, 17,* 279–301.

Kane, T. (2004). *The impact of after-school programs: Interpreting the results of four recent evaluations.* New York: William T. Grant Foundation.

Karp, K., & Howell, P. (2004). Building responsibility for learning in students with special needs. *Teaching Children Mathematics, 11,* 118–126.

Kinney, J. (2007). *Diary of a wimpy kid.* New York: Abrams Books for Young Readers.

Kluger, A. N., & DeNisi, A. (1996). The effects of feedback interventions on performance: A historical review, a meta-analysis, and a preliminary feedback intervention theory. *Psychological Bulletin, 119*(2), 254–284.

Krull, K. (1993). *Lives of the musicians: Good times, bad times (and what the neighbors thought).* San Diego, CA: Harcourt Brace & Company.

Krull, K. (1995). *Lives of the artists: Masterpieces, messes (and what the neighbors thought).* San Diego, CA: Harcourt Brace & Company.

Langer, G. M., Colton, A. B., & Goff, L. S. (2003). *Collaborative analysis of student work: Improving teaching and learning.* Alexandria, VA: ASCD.

Lapp, D., Fisher, D., Flood, J., & Cabello, A. (2000). An integrated approach to the teaching and assessment of language arts. In S. Hurley & J. Tinajero (Eds.), *Literacy assessment of second language learners* (pp. 1–26). Needham Heights, MA: Allyn and Bacon.

Lapp, D., Flood, J., & Goss, K. (2000). Desks don't move—students do: In effective classroom environments. *The Reading Teacher, 54*(1), 31–36.

LaPray, M., & Ross, R. (1969). The graded word list: Quick gauge of reading ability. *Journal of Reading, 12*(4), 305–307.

Leslie, L., & Allen, L. (1999). Factors that predict success in an early literacy intervention project. *Reading Research Quarterly, 34*(4), 404–424.

Leslie, L., & Caldwell, J. S. (2005). *Qualitative reading inventory—4.* Boston: Allyn and Bacon.

Locke, E. A., & Latham, G. P. (1990). *A theory of goal setting and task performance.* Englewood Cliffs, NJ: Prentice Hall.

Mager, E. W. (1999). The instructor/coach: How to know one when you see one. *Performance Improvement, 38*(2), 26–32.

Mallette, B., Maheady, L., & Harper, G. F. (1999). The effects of reciprocal peer coaching on preservice general educators' instruction of students with special learning needs. *Teacher Education and Special Education, 22*(4), 201–216.

Markow, D., Kim, A., & Liebman, M. (2007). *The MetLife survey of the American teacher: The homework experience.* New York: Metropolitan Life Insurance Company.

Mayo, D. (2001). *The house that Jack built.* New York: Barefoot Books.

McCormick, S. (1994). A nonreader becomes a reader: A case study of literacy acquisition by a severely disabled reader. *Reading Research Quarterly, 29,* 157–176.

Meyer, M. S. (2000). The ability-achievement discrepancy: Does it contribute to an understanding of learning disabilities? *Educational Psychology Review, 12*(3), 315–337.

Moody, S. W., Vaughn, S., & Schumm, J. S. (1997). Instructional grouping for reading: Teachers' views. *Remedial and Special Education, 18,* 347–356.

Morris, D., Ervin, C., & Conrad, K. (1996). A case study of middle school reading disability. *The Reading Teacher, 49,* 368–377.

Moss, L. (1995). *Zin! Zin! Zin! A violin.* New York: Simon & Schuster.

Muñoz, M. A., Potter, A. P., & Ross, S. M. (2008). Supplemental educational services as a consequence of the NCLB legislation: Evaluating its impact on student achievement in a large urban district. *Journal of Education for Students Placed at Risk, 13*(1), 1–25.

National Education Association. (2006). *New roles in response to intervention: Creating success for schools and children.* Available: www.nasponline.org/advocacy/New%20 Roles%20in%20RTI.pdf

Paris, S. G. (2005). Reinterpreting the development of reading skills. *Reading Research Quarterly, 40*(2), 184–202.

Parker, F. W. (1886). *The practical teacher.* New York: E. L. Kellogg.

Pearson, P. D., & Gallagher, G. (1983). The gradual release of responsibility model of instruction. *Contemporary Educational Psychology, 8,* 112–123.

Perkins, S. J. (1998). On becoming a peer coach: Practices, identities, and beliefs of inexperienced coaches. *Journal of Curriculum and Supervision, 13*(3), 235–254.

Pianta, R. C., Belsky, J., Houts, R., & Morrison, F. (2007). Opportunities to learn in America's elementary classrooms. *Science, 315,* 1795–1796.

Raschka, C. (2000). *Ring! Yo?* New York: Dorling Kindersley.

Rice, J. K. (1999). The impact of class size on instructional strategies and the use of time in high school mathematics and science courses. *Educational Evaluation and Policy Analysis, 21*(2), 215–229.

Riddle Buly, M., & Valencia, S.W. (2002). Below the bar: Profiles of students who fail state reading tests. *Educational Evaluation and Policy Analysis, 24,* 219–239.

Rubenstein-Avila, E. (2003/2004). Conversing with Miguel: An adolescent English language learner struggling with later literacy development. *Journal of Adolescent & Adult Literacy, 47,* 290–301.

Ryan, P. M. (2002). *When Marian sang.* New York: Scholastic.

Santa, C., & Havens, L. (1995). *Creating independence through student-owned strategies: Project CRISS.* Dubuque, IA: Kendall-Hunt.

Schmitt, M. C. (1990). A questionnaire to measure children's awareness of strategic reading processes. *The Reading Teacher, 43,* 454–461.

Shanahan, T., & Shanahan, C. (2008). Teaching disciplinary literacy to adolescents: Rethinking content-area literacy. *Harvard Educational Review, 78,* 40–59.

Simmons, D. C., Coyne, M. D., Kwok, O., McDonagh, S., Harn, B. A., & Kame'enui, E. J. (2008). Indexing response to intervention: A longitudinal study of reading risk from kindergarten to third grade. *Learning Disabilities Quarterly, 41*(2), 158–173.

Soldner, L. B. (1997). Self-assessment and the reflective reader. *Journal of College Reading and Learning, 28*(1), 5–11.

Steinbeck, J. (1939/2006). *The grapes of wrath*. New York: Penguin Classics.

Stichter, J. P., Stormont, M., & Lewis, T. J. (2009). Instructional practices and behavior during reading: A descriptive summary and comparison of practices in Title I and non-title elementary schools. *Psychology in the Schools, 46*(2), 172–183.

Studer, Q. (2003). *Hardwiring excellence: Purpose, worthwhile work, making a difference*. Gulf Breeze, FL: Fire Starter Publishing.

Summers, J. J. (2006). Effects of collaborative learning in math on sixth graders' individual goal orientations from a socioconstructivist perspective. *Elementary School Journal, 106,* 273–290.

Taylor, W. (1953). Cloze procedure: A new tool for measuring readability. *Journalism Quarterly, 30,* 414–438.

Tilly, W. D. (2008). Three tiers of intervention. *School Administrator, 65*(8), 20–23.

Tomlinson, C. A. (2001). *How to differentiate instruction in mixed-ability classrooms* (2nd ed.). Alexandria, VA: ASCD.

Tomlinson, C. A., & Strickland, C. A. (2005). *Differentiation in practice: A resource guide for differentiating curriculum, grades 9–12*. Alexandria, VA: ASCD.

Totten, S., Sills, T., Digby, A., & Russ, P. (1991). *Cooperative learning: A guide to research*. New York: Garland.

U.S. Department of Education. (2005). OSERS: Office of Special Education and Rehabilitation Services [home page]. Retrieved July 3, 2009, from www.ed.gov/about/offices/list/osers/index.html

U.S. Department of Education. (2009). 21st century community learning centers [home page]. Retrieved November 9, 2009, from www.ed.gov/programs/21stcclc/index.html

Vellutino, F. R., & Scanlon, D. M. (2001). Emergent literacy skills, early instruction, and individual differences as determinants of difficulties in learning to read: The case for early intervention. In S. B. Neuman & D. K. Dickinson (Eds.), *Handbook of early literacy research* (pp. 295–321). New York: The Guilford Press.

Vellutino, F. R., Scanlon, D. M., Small, S., & Fanuele, D. P. (2006). Response to intervention as a vehicle for distinguishing between children with and without reading disabilities: Evidence for the role of kindergarten and first-grade interventions. *Journal of Learning Disabilities, 39*(2), 157–169.

Vygotsky, L. S. (1978). *Mind in society* (M. Cole, V. John-Steiner, S. Scribner, & E. Souberman, Eds.). Cambridge, MA: Harvard University Press.

Walsh, J. A., & Sattes, B. D. (2005). *Quality questioning: Research-based practices to engage every learner.* Thousand Oaks, CA: Corwin.

Wasik, B. A., & Slavin, R. E. (1993). Preventing early reading failure with one-to-one tutoring: A review of five programs. *Reading Research Quarterly, 28,* 178–200.

Waters, T., Marzano, R. J., & McNulty, B. (2003). *Balanced leadership: What 30 years of research tells us about the effect of leadership on student achievement.* Aurora, CO: Mid-continent Research for Education and Learning. Available: www.mcrel.org/PDF/LeadershipOrganizationDevelopment/5031RR_BalancedLeadership.pdf

Weasmer, J., & Woods, A. M. (1999). Programs in practice: Peer partnering for change. *Kappa Delta Pi Record, 36*(1), 32–34.

Weitzman, J. P., & Glasser, R. P. (1998). *You can't take a balloon into the Metropolitan Museum.* New York: Dial Books for Young Readers.

Wigfield, A., & Eccles, J. S. (2002). *Development of achievement motivation.* San Diego, CA: Academic Press.

Wiggins, G., & McTighe, J. (2005). *Understanding by design* (2nd ed.). Alexandria, VA: ASCD.

Winerman, L. (2005). The mind's mirror. *Monitor on Psychology, 36*(9), 48–49.

Winograd, P., & Paris, S. G. (1989). A cognitive and motivational agenda for reading instruction. *Educational Leadership, 46*(4), 30–36.

Winter, J. (1998). *My name is Georgia.* San Diego, CA: Harcourt.

Winter, J. (2002). *Frida.* New York: Arthur A. Levine Books.

Wood, A. (1984). *The napping house.* San Diego, CA: Harcourt Brace & Company.

Worthy, J., & Broaddus, K. (2001/2002). Fluency beyond the primary grades: From group performance to silent, independent reading. *The Reading Teacher, 55,* 334–343.

Worthy, J., Broaddus, K., & Ivey, G. (2001). *Pathways to independence: Reading, writing, and learning in grades 3–8.* New York: The Guilford Press.

Worthy, J., Moorman, M., & Turner, M. (1999). What Johnny likes to read is hard to find in school. *Reading Research Quarterly, 34,* 12–27.

Index

Note: the letter *f* following a page number denotes a figure.

About the Authors

Douglas Fisher, PhD, is a professor of language and literacy education in the Department of Teacher Education at San Diego State University and a teacher at Health Sciences High & Middle College. He is the recipient of an International Reading Association Celebrate Literacy Award, the Paul and Kate Farmer Award for excellence in writing from the National Council of Teachers of English, and the Christa McAuliffe Award for excellence in teacher education. He is the author of numerous articles on reading and literacy, differentiated instruction, and curriculum design, and his published books include *Creating Literacy-Rich Schools for Adolescents* (with Gay Ivey), *Checking for Understanding: Formative Assessment Techniques for Your Classroom* (with Nancy Frey), *Better Learning Through Structured Teaching: A Framework for the Gradual Release of Responsibility* (with Nancy Frey), and *Content-Area Conversations: How to Plan Discussion-Based Lessons for Diverse Language Learners* (with Nancy Frey and Carol Rothenberg). He can be reached at dfisher@mail.sdsu.edu.

Nancy Frey, PhD, is a professor of literacy in the School of Teacher Education at San Diego State University (SDSU) and a teacher at Health Sciences High & Middle College. Nancy is a credentialed special educator and reading specialist in California. She is the recipient of the 2008 Early Career Achievement Award from the National Reading Conference and the Christa McAuliffe Award for excellence in teacher education from the American Association of State Colleges and Universities. She has published in *The Reading Teacher, Journal of Adolescent & Adult Literacy, English Journal, Voices*

in the Middle, Middle School Journal, Remedial and Special Education, and *Educational Leadership.* She has coauthored (with Doug Fisher) the ASCD books *Checking for Understanding, Better Learning Through Structured Teaching,* and *Content-Area Conversations.* She teaches a variety of courses in SDSU's teacher-credentialing and reading specialist programs on elementary and secondary reading instruction and literacy in content areas, classroom management, and supporting students with diverse learning needs. She can be reached at nfrey@mail.sdsu.edu.

Related ASCD Resources

At the time of publication, the following ASCD resources were available (ASCD stock numbers appear in parentheses). For up-to-date information about ASCD resources, go to www.ascd.org.

Networks

Visit the ASCD Web site (www.ascd.org) and search for "networks" for information about professional educators who have formed groups around topics like "Assessment for Learning," "Interdisciplinary Curriculum and Instruction," and "Quality Education." Look in the "Network Directory" for current facilitators' addresses and phone numbers.

Print Products

The Art and Science of Teaching: A Comprehensive Framework for Effective Instruction by Robert J. Marzano (#107001)

Better Learning Through Structured Teaching: A Framework for the Gradual Release of Responsibility by Douglas Fisher, Nancy Frey (#108010)

Collaborative Analysis of Student Work: Improving Teaching and Learning by Georgea M. Langer, Amy B. Colton, Loretta S. Goff (#102006)

Educating Everybody's Children: Diverse Teaching Strategies for Diverse Learners (revised and expanded 2nd edition) edited by Robert W. Cole (#107003)

Educational Leadership October 2007 Early Intervention at Every Age (#108021)

Getting to "Got It!": Helping Struggling Students Learn How to Read by Betty K. Garner (#107024)

Reframing Teacher Leadership to Improve Your School by Douglas B. Reeves (#108012)

What Every School Leader Needs to Know About RTI by Margaret Searle (#109097)

Videos

Breaking Through Barriers to Achievement (#605133)
How to Informally Assess Student Learning (#605121)
RTI in the Secondary Classroom and School (#610011)

The Whole Child Initiative helps schools and communities create learning environments that allow students to be healthy, safe, engaged, supported, and challenged. To learn more about other books and resources that relate to the whole child, visit www.wholechildeducation.org.

For more information: send e-mail to member@ascd.org; call 1-800-933-2723 or 703-578-9600, press 2; send a fax to 703-575-5400; or write to Information Services, ASCD, 1703 N. Beauregard St., Alexandria, VA 22311-1714 USA.